Making
College
PAY

Making
College
PAY

Strategies for Choosing Wisely, Doing Well & Maximizing Your Return

Alice C. Stewart
& Fran Stewart

Eagle Creek Press
Solon, Ohio

Eagle Creek Press
32513 Seneca Drive
Solon, OH 44139

ISBN: 978-0-9759366-9-6

Printed by BookMasters Inc., of Mansfield, Ohio.

Cover Illustration by Andrea Levy

To our parents – who modeled the joy of learning, taught the importance of pragmatism and showed that a family of modest means could send five kids to college.

Acknowledgments

We would like to thank Dr. Jacqueline Williams, Margaret Bernstein, Amy Benhoff Iosue, Kathy Baker, Jon Stewart, Pam Stewart, Toy Biederman and Holly Kitzmiller for their willingness to read and comment on versions of this manuscript. We also would like to thank Andrea Levy for her compelling cover illustration. We have attempted to make this discussion of college choice as numbers-based as possible. However, we hope you will forgive any errors in calculation, presentation or research.

I would like to acknowledge the support of my immediate and extended family for giving me the time, space, and encouragement to pursue this project. In particular, I'd like to thank Charlie Wilson for his love and support and his willingness to deal with our family challenges while I spent time at the computer working on this book and ignoring daily responsibilities! – Alice

I would like to thank my family – David, Eliot and Ethan Mook – for their support, indulgence and inspiration. – Fran

Contents

Part ONE:
The Big Picture

Key Concepts:
knowledge economy
global competition
earning potential

Chapter 1
Separating Fact From Fiction

Picture this scene: A working-class father gives up his own career and future to allow his daughter to achieve her dream of attending an elite college thousands of miles from home. He sells his small limousine business to come up with enough money to pay another year of tuition at a prestigious but pricey school so his daughter can "change the world" someday. The melodrama makes for great theater, helping propel the musical "In the Heights" to a Tony Award in 2008. Talk about art imitating life: The scene draws its power by mining the emotions surrounding one of the toughest and most confusing decisions families face today – college choice.

Note we said "families." Advice books and news articles often portray the choice as almost exclusively up to the students themselves. Parents are cast mostly in roles of emotional and financial support. It makes sense, right? Decisions about where to apply, how to get in and what to study are ones that directly affect students' futures. But such decisions also may have direct effect on the future of the entire family. That means the college decision isn't just about what you the student wants; it's about making choices that work for you and your family.

In the play, we're supposed to forget the fact that the father had originally rejected the low-ball purchase price for his business as insulting. Dismiss the fact that his daughter had already lost her scholarship and dropped out of school once before. Overlook the fact that selling the business to a developer would throw his employees out of work. Ignore the fact that there were probably a few dozen colleges – presumably with a lower price tag – within a 20-mile radius of the family's New York City neighborhood.

Such cold, hard facts seem downright petty compared to the dramatic idea of a parent sacrificing everything to give his child the best education possible. In the fictional "Heights," and often in the real world too, parents are applauded when inconvenient truths are ignored for rosy fantasies where everything, including picking a college without dealing with financial realities, "works out in the end." In this fantasy world, students and their parents are encouraged to believe that they can never overpay for a college degree and that having the family take on huge financial obligations will result in a secure and well-paying future for their eager young student.

If you are a typical college-bound high school student, you might have spent a lot of time worried about choosing the "right" school. Do you go for the top college you can get into or the one that gave you the warmest, fuzziest feeling the day you visited? Do you go where your friends go or do you strike off on your own? Your parents have likely divided their worries between hoping that the school you like likes you back and figuring out how to pay for your dream. Yet, if you are like countless other students, you probably have spent far less time pondering a really critical detail: How to make college pay off for you.

Consider this chapter's opening scene a perfect gut check of whether this book is for you. If you think the father made the right choice (without, by the way, even consulting his wife and business partner), you might as well stop reading now. You probably won't appreciate what we have to say.

If, on the other hand, you think the father's choice was, well, nuts (or, at the very least, ill-advised), then settle in and prepare for a frank, rational discussion about what has become a frenzied and irrational topic. Consider this conversation an antidote to the over-the-top, panic-inducing, you're-doomed-if-you-don't-make-it-into-the-best-school stories you read in the media, in other college advice books and even in schools' own admission materials. You'll find no hysterics here.

Wait, what's an advice book without at least some shrill warning? OK, so you'll find that we sound alarms in two key areas: taking on too much debt for an undergraduate degree and failing to graduate. Note we said *too much* debt. The warnings seem warranted given the facts:

- Only 57 percent of students who enroll full time at a four-year college actually graduate within *six* years.

- More than one-quarter of students who start college drop out before the second year.

- Two-thirds of four-year undergraduate students who actually make it to graduation leave college saddled with debt. On average, students who borrow owe $23,186, meaning they are looking at roughly a $230 monthly payment for at least 10 years. (By the way, this total is just for the students themselves. It *does not* include what parents might have borrowed.)

- Students who take out loans but never complete their college degrees are 10 times more likely to default on their loans and twice as likely to be unemployed as student borrowers who graduate.

Plenty of families every year are making choices about college without strategically thinking through the long-term benefits of the college degree and the long-term consequences of their financial commitments. Families get so caught up in the short-term thrill and pressure of the choice that they fail to think about the big picture.

As a result, too many families are paying more than they can afford or more than what makes economic sense for a college education, and too many students are leaving school – whether after graduating or dropping out – overburdened by debt yet lacking marketable skills.

That's right, the goal is *marketable* skills. While some young people may still seek a college degree for personal intellectual fulfillment, for the vast majority of students, getting a degree is really about getting a job. Many in higher education would be offended by our bluntness. College, they say, is about expanding the "life of the mind." In fact, higher education in the 21st century is about expanding your knowledge and skills so that you can compete in an increasingly competitive work environment. That means college is more of a business decision than a lifestyle choice.

Unfortunately, many students today are trapped between the old ways of thinking about college and the new realities of the competitive, technologically driven knowledge economy. Your college degree should give you some edge in the marketplace. That competitive advantage may come from a thoughtful understanding of world history and economic systems or from a thorough grasp of the latest breakthrough in biotechnology. But whatever area of knowledge and skill development you choose, you need to be aware that the economic value of a college education is directly related to the value of the knowledge and skills you gain. And the economic value of the knowledge and skills you gain is, for good or bad, determined by the marketplace. If you accept that basic premise, then you're ready to plan an education investment strategy that makes the most of your knowledge and financial capital.

Why the College Decision
Is Different in the 21st Century

If you've ever heard the phrase "knowledge economy," then you already know why the decision to go to college is different today than it was a generation ago. The knowledge economy refers to the fact that brain beats brawn in the economic marketplace of the 21st century. There are a lot of ways to join the knowledge economy, but most young people have figured out that a college degree is one of the most direct routes to a prosperous future.

Unfortunately, most advice about college hasn't changed to keep up with the times. What kind of college, how much to spend and how to invest your time once you get on campus are the decisions that cause many students and parents to flounder. What we hope to do with this book is help you get the most out of this first big life choice. But first, let's talk about why the decision to go to college is so different now. *In a nutshell, the enrollment numbers are higher, the costs are higher, the stakes are higher, but the financial, social and developmental rewards may not be.*

Difference No. 1: Huge numbers of people go to college now, not just the academic and financial elite.

Higher education was never set up to prepare large numbers of people to compete in a global marketplace. In your parents' generation, only about 20 percent of people who completed high school went on to earn a bachelor's degree. (Sixty years ago, only about 5 percent of all U.S. adults had a bachelor's degree.) The people who went on to college back then tended to be students who had the best academic preparation, the most money or an extraordinary amount of personal motivation. Today, close to 70 percent of high school graduates plan to continue their education. Many of these students are not attending college because they want to explore the "life of the mind." Instead, the vast majority head off to college these days because that is what they believe they must do to land a good-paying job. This means that college is increasingly seen as "vocational" or work preparation, not a hallowed "ivory tower" of theoretical learning.

The growing number of people participating in undergraduate education has put a lot of pressure on colleges and universities, which don't always know how to help students from an increasingly wider variety of academic and financial backgrounds succeed and make it to graduation. In many ways, the traditional structure of higher education has not adapted to what has been a seismic shift in college participation. How do we know this? Recall that earlier graduation statistic: Among those students who enroll full-time at a four-year college after high school, *only 57 percent succeed in earning a degree from that school within six years,* according to the most recent National Center for Education Statistics data. That means 43 percent dropped out somewhere along the way, whether after one year or after five. The appalling reality in the rosy college picture is that far too few students realize any actual return on their family's college investment. Here's the shocker: **If you leave college without earning a degree, you will see very little economic benefit from your education investment.**

What Does This Mean for You?

To increase your chances of success in college, it is more important than ever to make sure that the college or university you choose is the best option for you in the long run. You have to think more strategically about the reason you are going to college, what you plan to get from the experience and what your priorities are.

Difference No. 2: College is expensive.

The second reason that the decision to go to college is different in the 21st century is the cost. College costs have been increasing dramatically. For the past 30 years, the sticker price for attending college has increased much faster than the costs of other goods and services, according to the College Board's "Trends in College Pricing 2010." Even controlling for inflation, the average published tuition price of a four-year public university is now *3.5 times* what it was in 1980. The average published price for tuition and fees at a private college is now nearly *3 times* what it was 30 years ago. In the past 10 years alone, the published price for tuition and fees at a four-year public university has grown, on average, by about *7 percent each year.*

According to the College Board report, the average annual published price for attending a public institution tops *$16,000 per year.* This price includes tuition, fees, room and board. The average published price for private not-for-profit institutions is nearly *$37,000 per year. When you add it all up, a four-year degree comes with an average sticker price of **$64,000** to **$148,000.***

We should point out that most students do not pay the sticker price. About two-thirds receive some sort of financial aid. A 2010 report from the National Center for Education

What Does This Mean for You?

Unless you have your own private stash of cash, coming up with the cost of four years' worth of a college education will require some strategic thinking. Getting the best deal and the biggest bang for your buck should be a top priority. That's how you improve the odds that your investment of time, money and hard work will pay off. As you'll see, not all college investments are created equal.

Definitions

Public – Public institutions can be universities, colleges, community colleges or technical schools. Public means that the state where the school is located subsidizes part of the total cost of the education for the benefit of the state's citizens. This is why "in-state" tuition is almost always lower than "out-of-state" tuition and why public school tuition is almost always lower than private school tuition. Some states have a lot of public institutions and have a lot invested in higher education at all levels: community colleges, regional colleges and universities, and research universities. Other states may have only a few publicly supported universities.

Private – Private institutions can be universities, colleges or technical schools. Private means that these schools do not receive state funding, so they must pay all their bills based on the money they earn through tuition, fees, and other sources (such as endowments and grants). This is why the tuition at these schools is so much higher. For a private school, there is no distinction between a student from the same state or one from another state regarding tuition. Most private institutions are not-for-profit.

Statistics found that when grants were subtracted out, the net price to students attending a four-year public institution was about $15,000 per year, and the net price to students attending a private, not-for profit institution was about $26,000 per year. That's a significant discount off the published price, but it's still a substantial cost.

Difference No. 3: Without advanced education and skill building, you will be less competitive in a global, wired economy.

In his best-selling book *The World Is Flat, New York Times* columnist Thomas Friedman wrote of the growing importance of advanced education and training if U.S. workers are to be competitive against well-trained, well-educated workers throughout the world. The major economies that are joining the United States at the center of the economic stage are China and India. The 21st century global economy is increasingly a numbers game, and the numbers alone are going to raise the stakes for young American workers in ways that many of us can't even imagine. Even with a college degree, competing on the global stage is more difficult all the time. In a globalized economy, the numbers are stacked against us – and here's why.

China has about 1.3 billion people. That's about four times more people than the United States has. India has about 1.1 billion people (more than three times more people than the United States has, many of whom speak English). Together, China and India have at least 2.4 *billion* people compared to the 311 *million* people in the United States. What does this have to do with college today? We'll show you. Let's assume that about 20 percent of any group of people represent "the really, really smart group." In the United States, this would be about 62 million people. But think about it – and use your high school math. The top 20 percent of China and India combined, their "really, really

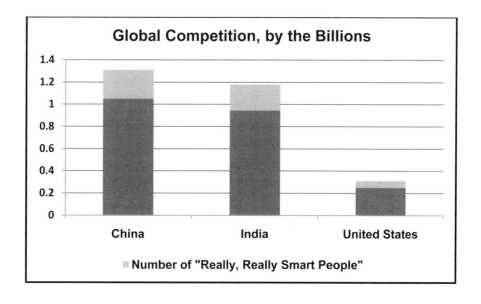

Global Competition, by the Billions

Number of "Really, Really Smart People"

smart group," would be about 480 million people. *That's more than the entire U.S. population!* So the "average" people in the United States (the other 80 percent of us) are going to be competing head-to-head in the global economy with the top 20 percent of these two new economic competitors for jobs, for entrepreneurial financing, for economic life.

What Does This Mean for You?

For starters, whether you're a great student or an "average" one, you should understand that advanced education — whether that is a bachelor's degree, an associate's degree, a professional degree, a certificate program or an apprenticeship — helps you stay ahead of the curve in this VERY competitive global environment. It's up to you and your generation to leverage the higher educational system in the United States to get ahead and stay ahead in the 21st century marketplace.

But, you may think, they are over there and we are over here. Sorry! The wired, globally networked, 24/7 world means that people in Chennai, India, can do some of the exact same jobs (such as writing software, doing taxes, creating graphic designs) as someone in Chicago, Illinois. When your parents and grandparents were starting their work lives, they typically only had to compete with other workers in their own neighborhoods. In some industries, they might have competed with workers across the state or even the nation. In general, competition was more limited and more localized. For your generation, competition is unlimited and globalized.

Now, before you start thinking that globalization has just made things harder for you (which it has), it also has brought, and will continue to bring, opportunity. But you need to have the right skills to seize that opportunity. This is one reason why advanced education is more important for you than it may have been for your parents or grandparents.

The challenge of competing head-to-head with such large numbers of smart, talented workers from the other side of the world is daunting. Yet, American young people do have an edge: higher education. China and India are still in the process of developing their higher education infrastructure, while the U.S. system of higher education is, for now, considered among the best in the world. Access to that system provides a competitive advantage. If you don't believe us, ask all the Chinese and Indian students who come to the United States every year to attend college and gain an educational edge in the 21st century global marketplace.

Difference No. 4: The long-term value of an undergraduate college education isn't as high as it used to be.

We can't overstate the importance of being educated beyond the high school level if you are hoping to find a good-paying job in the global knowledge economy of the 21st century. But here is another reality check: As the number of college-educated workers increases, the financial value of a bachelor's degree is likely to *decrease*. At least in terms of earning potential, the standard four-year degree may lose the differentiating punch that it traditionally has had.

This has happened before. Back in the 1970s, the number of college graduates increased as governments promoted greater access to higher education; as a result, the average salary paid to new college graduates decreased relative to what earlier graduates had earned. And the number of students going to college back in the '70s was nowhere near as high as it is today. According to the National Center for Education Statistics, in 1972, about 49 percent of students who completed high school started college the following fall. That translates into about 1.5 million college freshmen. By 2008, 69 percent of students,

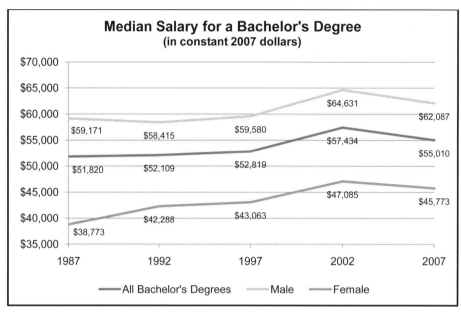

Median Salary for a Bachelor's Degree
(in constant 2007 dollars)

Source: National Center for Education Statistics

or 2.2 million, entered college immediately after graduating high school.

Jobs in the 21st century increasingly demand education beyond high school, but as the four-year college degree becomes more and more common, employers will not pay higher salaries just because you happen to have one. In other words, a bachelor's degree in the 21st century is becoming a commodity. (In economic terms, a commodity refers to something so widely available that its profit margin has shrunk.) Not having a degree is a huge disadvantage, but just having a degree won't give you as much of a competitive edge as it used to. So the difficult truth of the 21st century is that a college degree is more necessary than it has ever been but, at the same time, the potential financial rewards in the marketplace are likely to be lower than they used to be.

As you can see from the graph, the value of a bachelor's degree hit its highest point (in constant 2007 dollars) in 2002 and then began to fall steadily. With the difficult

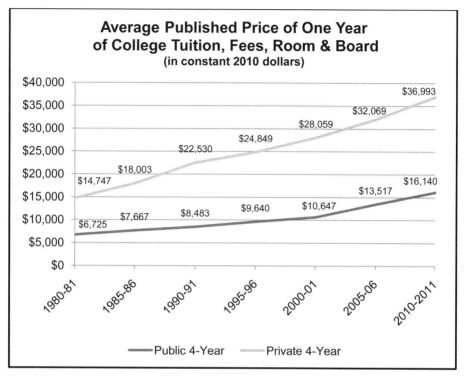

**Average Published Price of One Year
of College Tuition, Fees, Room & Board
(in constant 2010 dollars)**

Source: CollegeBoard.com. "Trends in College Pricing, 2010"

economy of the past few years, there is no expectation that the decline in value will turn around anytime soon. If you look over time, the value of a bachelor's degree (in constant dollars) has gone up only 6 percent in *20 years!*

Compare that to the change in tuition, fees, and room and board prices at most colleges and universities over that same time period. *The average undergraduate rate charged for a full-time year of college is now nearly 90 percent more (in constant 2010 dollars) than it was for the 1986-1987 academic year.*

Just for fun, let's look at how the increase in the cost of college stacks up against price changes for other common items. Now, we admit this isn't a perfect comparison. But we think it does give you some sense of how out of whack the price of a year of college has become. As you can see in the next chart, the nearly 90 percent inflation-adjusted

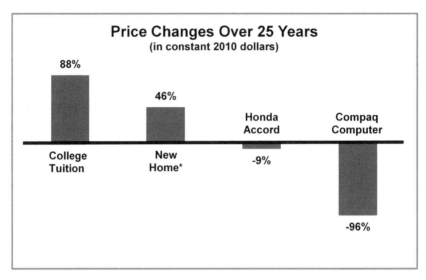

Price Changes Over 25 Years
(in constant 2010 dollars)

88% — College Tuition
46% — New Home*
-9% — Honda Accord
-96% — Compaq Computer

Source: National Center for Education Statistics; U.S. Census Bureau; Bureau of Labor Statistics, Consumer Price Index
*The percentage change in the median price of a new house is from March 1987 to March 2007, which represents the peak price for housing. Average tuition, fees, room and board are from 1986-1987 to 2009-2010.

increase in the average rate charged for a year of tuition, fees, room and board at a four-year college or university is substantially greater than the ballooning of new home prices. From March 1987 to March 2007 (when the housing "bubble" was still fully inflated), the median price for a new house rose by about 46 percent, in constant dollars.

The inflation-adjusted cost of a 2010 Honda Accord has actually declined by about 9 percent compared to the nearly $13,000 price tag for a 1986 LXi sedan. That decline in "real" cost may come as a welcome surprise to your parents if they're looking for a reliable family car, but it pales in comparison to the massive drop in computer pricing. In 1987, a Compaq III portable computer would have set you back nearly $5,800 for what was then a robust 40 megabyte hard drive and 640k RAM in a clunky 20-pound package. In 2010, a Compaq Presario Notebook PC will set you back little more than $500 for a 320 gigabyte hard drive in a sleek 5-pound laptop. The astounding decrease in price, combined with an equally astounding increase in computing power, illustrates the incredible value proposition of advanced technology.

The skyrocketing cost of a bachelor's degree makes it hard to state such a confident value claim about higher education. Yes, college is an investment in your future. Census Bureau data show that workers with a bachelor's degree earn, on average, 60 percent more than workers with only a high

rese

mar

of l

var

suc

bet

edu

mo

What Does This Mean for You?

Students who are trying to choose their college path would be wise to consider some very practical advice: Look for ways to reduce the cost of education and raise its value. If you think about college as an investment in your future and carefully calculate your expected return on that investment, you stand to make better, more practical choices that will provide u with the future opportunities u want.

lower obesity rates, to with higher levels of mployed and tend to be

its. However, there is a ver oversimplified message high school students often hear about the importance and value of college. The rewarding payback for your investment of money and time to earn a bachelor's degree is nowhere near the "sure bet" it once was. An increasingly complex set of variables is changing the college choice calculus. That means you are going to need some different strategies and different tools to help you make choices about education so that you will be rewarded in the 21st century marketplace.

How This Book Is Organized

College should give students a competitive advantage in the marketplace. In many ways, it's a business decision that requires a strategic approach. We admittedly are taking a more pragmatic perspective than most college advice books. We believe that, when you make decisions about your academic future, you should give less weight to emotion and more weight to the value of your financial investment relative to your future prospects. That's what Part One of this book aims to help you and your family do: gain the understanding and perspective you need to make choices that maximize the return on your college investment. That means making choices that focus on three goals:

- *Minimize costs.*

- *Increase marketability.*

- *Improve the likelihood of graduation.*

In Chapter 2, we provide an overview of the three goals. In Chapter 3, we introduce you to the idea of our College Payback Ratio. (Yes, we chose the acronym CPR deliberately to call your attention to how this critical step may save you from making a life-limiting choice.) We walk you through some examples of college offers that reflect very different investment profiles. In Chapter 4, we discuss how you can lower the "investment" piece of the CPR by taking a wider and more pragmatic view of your college options. Chapter 5 looks at how your decisions about your major affect your potential financial returns. Chapter 6 offers advice about taking on debt to pay for your college education. It's sometimes necessary, but we want to make sure you understand the big-picture implications. In Chapter 7, we give you some practical advice about how to avoid common college pitfalls and what to do to increase your chances of graduating in a reasonable amount of time.

Part Two of this book helps you analyze potential college choices and decipher some of the key pieces of information that tell you a lot about a college or university. Chapter 8 helps you understand how differences in the data that you find about colleges and universities may affect your success as a student. Chapter 9 focuses on you and your individual situation. We give you a framework to help you think about the type of institution that will help you meet the three goals we discuss in Part One. Chapter 10 walks you through a free source for all sorts of information about different colleges. We then show you how to make sense of all that data.

Part Three brings us back to the big picture again. Chapter 11 discusses how to increase the market value of your college portfolio by focusing on "know-how" rather than "know-what." Chapter 12 acknowledges something that most people in the college business don't want to talk about: the fact that not everyone should go to college. In Chapter 13, we examine the necessity of lifelong learning. We end by providing a few worksheets to encourage you to apply what you have learned.

We hope that this book can give you some tips and insight that will help you and your family plan for the next four, six or more years of educational investment. It's time to get started!

Cram Session

- Young people like you face a higher education paradox: A college degree is more important today than ever before for you to land a good-paying job. However, as more people graduate college, the earning potential of your college degree is likely to go down.

- Far too many students receive little or no payoff from their higher education investment because they leave college without finishing or they take on too much debt.

Key Concepts:
avocation *vs.* vocation
professional development
personal development
marketability

Chapter 2
The Three Main Goals

When all those slick, glossy brochures begin to arrive in your mailbox, maintaining a cool, rational, business approach to the college choice process is difficult. Everything looks so perfect and so desirable. Each admissions packet is deliberately crafted to make you think that days are always sunny, co-eds are always beautiful, faculty are always kind and helpful, and college is four years of basketball, basket weaving and bonding. What's not to like? Less time in classrooms than high school, more options for fun on campus, 24-hour pizza delivery – and no parents.

As lovely as the images may seem, those glossy photos and slick brochures downplay just how hard it is for students to succeed during the college years. From our perspective, success isn't just getting the grades in the classroom; it's getting the degree and making a transition to the real world that won't leave you right back in your parents' house a few years down the road.

It's not the easiest thing to do, but even now, as you are poised at the start of this new adventure, *you have to keep the big picture in mind.* One mistake young people make is that they don't think *strategically* about the college decision. Far too often, students focus a lot of time on the decision of which school or what major. Then, after the pressure of the big choice is over, students get sucked into the day-today, week-to-week, semester-to-semester rhythm of college and forget about the big picture of why they are there in the first place.

Focusing on just the next step in front of us is how many of us get through life. Keeping an eye on the bigger picture is not what we do. It doesn't help that college life is broken down into chunks that make it so easy to focus on the short run. Semesters, football season, basketball season, homecoming, spring fling – you move from one thing to the other. Trust us, in college, there is always something to do. It's hard to keep the big picture in mind when there is so much to distract you every day. This is why it is important for you to visualize what you want your future to look like *before* you ever set foot on campus. Now, this doesn't mean that you should expect your future to look exactly like what you envisioned. Life doesn't work that way. But if you and your family can think through some of the big-picture issues now, *before* you make a commitment, *before* you "fall in love" with a pretty campus, *before* your parents add a second mortgage to the house, you can improve the odds that your college investment will be a good one.

In general, you should have three core goals for your college experience: Minimize costs. Increase marketability. Improve the likelihood of graduation. Whatever choice you make about where to go and what to study, consider how your decisions and actions will help or hinder your progress toward accomplishing these three goals.

Goal 1: Minimize Costs

Be a savvy shopper. Whatever you decide to do after high school, don't overspend. It is easy to be swayed by the admissions recruiters who are selling (yes, that is the right word) you on the uniqueness of their college. They are trying to persuade you that the four years you spend there will be worth the price and that the experience their college or university offers will open doors to your future in ways that can't be replicated anywhere else. Just like a car sales associate, they can "help" you figure out how to find the cash to close the deal. And like car sales staff and real estate agents, they are really skilled at the "up-sell," getting you to buy more than you really wanted or thought you could afford.

It's true that some college and university locations are really picturesque and wonderful. Some have exciting athletic programs. And some have invested in special services, such as concierges and afternoon ice cream. But the cold, hard truth is that, plus or minus some bells and whistles, most college *programs* (meaning majors, requirements, curricula, etc.) *are pretty much the same.* If you drill down into some of the admissions information that doesn't come dressed in attractive trappings, you are likely to find that the *academic* requirements and courses in majors are quite similar. Let's give you an example from a common degree – Business Administration.

On the next page, we list program requirements pulled from two real universities. The

Strategy Tip

On the college visit, ask about career services and corporate recruitment on campus. This is one place where an individual college may add value. This is also one place where the college "brand" might pay off. There is a BIG difference between a school that has a state-of-the-art Career Services Center and hosts on-campus career fairs and schools that don't.

Here are some questions you should consider: Does the Career Services Office offer electronic portfolios and places for students to post their resumes and work products online? Do the career fairs attract large companies that you may have heard of? Are the companies local, regional or national? Does the center appear to have sufficient staffing for a university of its size? Do the people look "professional" in their dress and in their interactions?

If all you see is a student worker and piles of resume books, you should think carefully about whether that school has the resources to get you on your way to the career payoff you want.

Namebrand University

General Education Requirements
English Composition and Rhetoric (6 hours)
Foreign Language (7 hours)
Quantitative Reasoning (3 hours)
Lifetime Fitness (1 hour)
Physical and Life Sciences (7 hours)
Social and Behavioral Sciences (9 hours)
Humanities and Fine Arts (9 hours)
Philosophical and Moral Reasoning (3 hours)
Visual, Performing and Literary Arts (6 hours)

Major: Core Courses for Bachelor of Science in Business Administration (all courses 3 credit hours)
MATH 152 Calculus
ECON 101 Introduction to Economics
ECON410 Microeconomics
BUSI 100 Financial Accounting
BUSI 101 Management Accounting
BUSI 401 Management Communication
BUSI 403 Operations Management
BUSI 404 Legal & Ethical Environment of Business
BUSI 405 Organizational Behavior
BUSI 406 Principles of Marketing
BUSI 407 Financial Statement Analysis
BUSI 408 Finance
BUSI 410 Business Analytical Applications
BUSI 698 Strategic Management

Majors (Remaining course requirements vary by topic)
Consulting
Entrepreneurial Studies
Finance
International Business
Investments
Marketing Consulting
Marketing Management
Real Estate
Sales

Neverheardofit University

General Education Requirements
Writing I (100 level) (3 hours)
Writing II (200 level) (3 hours)
Fundamentals of Speech (3 hours)
Math Reasoning (3 hours)
Computer Competence (3 hours)
Humanities (9 hours)
Natural and Mathematical Science (9 hours)
Social and Behavioral Sciences (9 hours)
Practical Living (3 hours)

Bachelor in Business Administration (all 3 credit hour courses)
ACCT 281 Financial Accounting
ACCT 282 Managerial Accounting
ECON 201 Macroeconomics
ECON 202 Microeconomics
MNGT 160 Business in Today's Society
MNGT 261 Legal Environment of Business
BIS 321 Business Communications
BIS 421 Business & Technical Presentations
CIS 311 Management Information Systems
ECON/MNGT 300 Quantitative Methods in Business and Economics
FIN 360 Business Finance
MKT 304 Marketing
MNGT 301 Principles of Management
MNGT 465 Organizational Behavior
MNGT 499C Strategic Management
MSU 400 World of Work
Any ECON Course above 300 level

Majors (Remaining course requirements vary by topic)
Accounting
Business Information Technology Education
Computer Information Systems
Economics
Finance
Management (General)
Marketing
Small Business Management & Entrepreneurship
General Business
Management (International)
Sport Management

Namebrand University is consistently rated as one of the top undergraduate business programs in the country. Neverheardofit University is a small regional campus in a rural area of a small state. As you can see, while there are some differences, the actual courses that you might take have some striking similarities. You have to keep in mind that a lot of colleges have the same accrediting agencies, try to attract the same employers to their career services, and have faculty who get their doctorates from the same types of schools. Although there are always going to be differences across campuses, those differences may not be as great as you think, given the differences in price tags. The differences may have little to do with the actual knowledge that you are supposed to acquire with the degree.

Think outside the classroom. Some schools like to tout various opportunities, such as service learning, study abroad, undergraduate research and internships. But these offerings are currently hot trends in higher education, so large numbers of colleges and universities have many of the same kinds of extra- or co-curricular elements. Before you buy into the "uniqueness" of these amenities, be a smart shopper and ask a few questions: How many students actually take advantage of these extracurricular opportunities? Will you be expected to come up with extra cash to take advantage of the opportunity? Will the experience put you behind in your major coursework and increase the amount of time needed to graduate?

Although many are willing to pay extra for a "brand name," do you really want to pay a premium when the product is essentially the same? Don't get lured into paying more than the academic product is worth to you. Think carefully about which services and opportunities you're likely to take advantage of and which may be bells and whistles you will never use. What are you willing to pay for? If you can save $20,000 on tuition, maybe you can afford the semester in Spain or the eco-tour to Costa Rica.

> **Definitions**
> **Co-curricular** refers to school-sponsored activities that are likely to enhance your professional development. Examples include internships and study-abroad programs. **Extracurricular** activities enhance your social development (for example, social clubs and intramural athletics) and might be just for fun. In some colleges and universities, co-curricular activities are tracked and presented with your academic transcript. Future employers tend to be more impressed with co-curricular rather than extracurricular activities.

Keep debt in perspective and under control. Some college admissions counselors, with the most sincere and heartfelt expression imaginable and without once choking on the number, will assure you that spending $100,000 or more on a bachelor's degree is completely normal and reasonable for middle-income families. What the counselor won't say is that because most middle-income families don't have college trust funds and can't tap into an inheritance, the student, and his or her family, usually will have to incur debt in order to make the college dream come true.

Debt isn't evil. It can get you where you need to go. It can also get you in a load of trouble. We'll even go a bit further. The way debt has been pushed on college students and their families over the past several years *is* evil. Debt can be seductive. Borrowing can be habit-forming. If you don't believe us, think about our nation's consumer debt, which stood at $2.4 trillion at the end of 2010, with about $800 billion of that in the form of revolving credit card debt. Keep in mind that college students are usually beginners at managing their own money, add in that the time to pay back the money seems a long way off, and remember the heady – sometimes even intoxicated – environment of college, and you can see how easy it is to forget about the ugly realities of a long and expensive repayment plan. In 2010, the website

Finaid.org released a sobering finding: Total student loan debt had exceeded total U.S. credit card debt for the first time ever.

This isn't what you will hear from many admissions counselors, but here is the big-picture point of view: *You should only take on as much debt as you can reasonably expect to repay.* To make it easy for you to visualize, we offer this rule of thumb: Take on no more total debt for your *entire* undergraduate degree than you would be willing to pay for a new car. If you or your parents think that taking out a $60,000 or $80,000 loan for a luxury car is an outrageous waste of money for a young, unemployed adult, then why would it make sense for a high-end, overpriced bachelor's degree? Sure, unlike a car, education is an investment. The $23,000 debt you might expect to incur while earning a degree and learning marketable skills is going to be much, much, much more valuable in the long run than the $23,000 you could plunk down on a 2010 Chevy Camaro Coupe. *But admissions counselors want you to think that you can never overpay for education. Don't believe them.*

Strategy Tip

Let's run some real numbers on college debt. At 8 percent interest on $65,000 in student loans, you can expect a monthly payment of nearly $789. The interest alone will total $29,635 over the life of the loan. The Project on Student Debt has determined that $65,000 in student loans at 8 percent interest over 10 years is unmanageable for any individual earning less than $70,000 annually. According to the Project on Student Debt report, even a more typical debt level of $25,000 is unmanageable at an annual income of under $40,000. Even if you earn $40,000 as your starting salary, you will be using more than 9 percent of your pretax earnings to repay your loan, which would likely affect other choices in your life, such as buying a house, getting married or going to graduate school.

Goal 2: Increase Marketability

Avocation or vocation? There's a difference between the job you would love to do and the job that some employer is willing to pay you to do. That distinction is the difference between avocation and vocation. After years in the working world, parents know this, but they rarely are able to convince their college-bound student of the fact. After an initial "you want to study what?" parents typically get on board and encourage their children's pursuit of passions. Really, who wants to stand in the way of people doing what they love? Isn't that what Oprah tells us to do? We certainly aren't going to stand in your way – *provided, of course, that you understand that intellectual pursuits and marketable skills don't necessarily go hand-in-hand.* Don't believe us? Then why are there so many art history and comparative literature graduates selling cars, managing boutiques and working other jobs outside their fields?

Now, before you start thinking that we're soulless pragmatists who care only about monetary reward, we love art and poetry and theater as much as anyone. If you have a passion that feeds your soul, we commend you. We wish more students experienced a thirst for meaning, beauty, creativity or expression like yours. That kind of zeal enriches the world. But unless you're uniquely talented or extraordinarily lucky, this passion may feed your soul, but it may not feed your family.

Here's where the compromise comes in. We want you to consider the possibility that a good college experience can accommodate both avocation and vocation. There are plenty of elements in a college degree, including things like electives, certificates, minors and concentrations. These elements are built into most college curricula. The political science junkie might focus on a particular area, such as health care or economics, to gain some knowledge and expertise that will enhance marketability in the long run.

The art major might go after a concentration in management just in case working for a major art museum or running a gallery provides a better living than sculpting. Chemistry majors might add some courses in forensic science. Vocational preparation is a reality. College isn't simply about the life of the mind; it also must sustain the life of the rest of the body in the long run. When you graduate, you have to eat!

Personal development or professional development?
If you keep the big picture in mind, you will see that there is a connection between Goal 1 and Goal 2. Making sure you are marketable upon graduation gives you just a touch more room to maneuver in making your college choices. In a difficult job market, students who have worked on their professional development as well as their personal development have an edge over their classmates.

In the transition time between your high school world and the real world, you grow and change in many ways. Research shows that the brains of people between the ages of 18 and 28 are continuing to develop in areas associated with judgment and critical thinking. Even if you don't go to college, you will see the world differently as a twenty-something than you do as an 18-year-old. So while college is a place of intellectual challenge and development, some amount of personal development will probably happen regardless of the institution you choose for your bachelor's degree.

If personal development is a given, professional development is not. Students generally don't start thinking about professional development until about their senior year of college, when the time comes to start thinking about a job. At that point, the resume can look pretty thin. Trust us, when the time comes, your experiences in intramural flag football or as fraternity chug champion won't help you stand out on the interview list – at least not in a good way.

So what can you do? Here is the big-picture perspective: *Just as you think about a college degree as being a four-year experience, you need to think of your personal and professional development as a four-year process, as well.* You want to make sure that your college experiences build on each other and that you develop a variety of skill sets.

This "co-curricular" development is why colleges and universities push things like study abroad, internships and service learning. These activities are supposed to provide you with experiences that will broaden your perspective, develop your self-reliance and enhance your skills at working creatively in teams. Regardless of your field of study, maturity, self-reliance and teamwork are always going to be valued in the marketplace. These are skills that can enrich you both personally and professionally. Experiences that help you develop these skills will make you more marketable *and* provide a more interesting college career.

Although you will find plenty of opportunity for developmental experiences in college, making sure that you have experiences that also improve your marketability takes some effort. Many schools now play up opportunities for international study, internships and undergraduate research in their informational brochures, but if you were to ask the typical college graduate whether he or she did any of these things, the answer would likely to be "no." So it's not automatic. You have to be proactive in taking advantage of the opportunities that are available. Maybe you don't feel like you are the type to study in China or do a summer internship in inner-city Chicago. But these are just the kinds of experiences that put you ahead rather than behind the pack.

Coursework can only take you so far. Employers are

looking for more than just a checklist of classes. A lot of learning occurs when you stretch yourself beyond your comfort zone. College is a fairly safe place to try things that help you understand your strengths and your weaknesses, help you figure out what makes you crazy and what makes you creative, and allow you to explore your ability to operate under pressure and work with others who are not like you. Internships, student organizations, study abroad and research are all ways to learn new skills *and* learn about yourself. While these things enhance marketability, they also enhance *you*.

Goal 3: Improve the Likelihood of Graduation

The only way a college experience pays off is if you get the degree. A 2004 report from the Pell Institute for the Study of Opportunity in Higher Education found that: "In some ways, leaving college before graduating is a greater liability than never having attended. The majority of research on the economic returns from college suggests that the earning power of a student who does not complete college is roughly equivalent to that of a high school graduate. ... In addition, the non-completing student has likely forgone income to attend college, and may be burdened with a loan payment that will reduce his or her income even further."

We'll state it in simpler terms: *If you choose to go to college, you have to commit to finishing or you will see little to no benefit. Taking on debt and failing to graduate does you much more harm than good.*

We define "finishing" as being awarded a bachelor's degree in some subject area within a six-year timeframe (four years would be even better). "Of course I'll finish," you're probably thinking, "I wouldn't even be going unless I planned to finish!" We are absolutely sure that is your intent, but the facts tell a different story. The numbers regarding the probability of graduating are sobering and should warrant more attention from parents, high school counselors and college advisers.

As we mentioned before, of 100 students who start college, only 57 of them, on average, will complete a degree at their chosen school within six years. This means that if four friends start at the same college, probably only two of them will actually graduate with a bachelor's degree within six years. There are a lot of reasons why students can't make it to the finish line. Some reasons are financial, which is why we keep emphasizing the importance of paying attention to how much this experience is going to cost. Some reasons are academic. Many students find themselves in over their heads when they get to college. Although it's true that for a given major, curricula across various colleges and universities are often similar, there is still a lot of variance in terms of what goes on inside any given classroom. Some colleges have a culture that is quite demanding, while others have more modest intellectual objectives for their student body. It is important that you know both whether you are likely to fit financially *and* academically at the schools in which you are interested. Finding the type of college that fits *your* profile and *your* needs is critical to increasing the probability that you graduate. We'll talk more about this in Part 2.

A Reality Check

If you can keep these three goals in mind, you will improve your odds of making good choices regarding college. The goals themselves seem simple enough, but in reality, it is often difficult to balance all three goals simultaneously. Usually, you can satisfy two of the goals, but you may have to sacrifice the third in the process. For example, you might pick a college or university that minimizes your cost and has an academic profile that improves the likelihood that you will persist to graduation. Focusing on those goals might mean that you have to give up a little on the goal of marketability. Maybe to keep costs down, you can't afford to study abroad or do an unpaid internship. Maybe the school you pick doesn't attract the best corporate recruiters.

Another possibility is that you really go for a challenging academic fit with lots of bells and whistles that will provide an excellent personal and professional development experience. However, it will cost you. The price tag might require that you exceed the family budget and take on more debt than is comfortable. To justify that excessive debt, you'll need to commit to maximizing every advantage, but it can be the right choice in the right circumstances. Just realize that when you get out, you will have much less flexibility in terms of choices about your job. You may need to take that corporate entry-level position with the fast-track career instead of taking time off to travel or do volunteer work in Africa.

So what is the best balance? What is the best choice? How do you weigh the options? Here's our view of the best choice for you: The best fit would be the one that allows you to achieve all three goals. But, unlike many other college advice books, we know that "best" is an elusive, idealized notion. In other words, it's often not reality. The reality is that life is about trade-offs. We just ask that you make these trade-offs with a clear eye to your future, an understanding of what you may gain and what you may have to give up, and a healthy appreciation for the big picture and the long-term implications of your choices.

Cram Session

- When you and your family sit down to make a choice about college, evaluate each option in terms of how it enables you to achieve three goals: Minimize your cost. Increase your marketability. Improve your odds of graduating.

- If you want to have an edge over your classmates when you get out into the marketplace, look for opportunities on campus to work on your professional development as well as your personal development.
- If you choose to go to college, you have to commit to finishing or you will see little to no benefit.

Key Concepts:
College Payback Ratio
education investment
Marginal Market Value

Chapter 3
Calculating the College Payback Ratio

We know that the college choice isn't *all* about money, but, at the end of the day, if you don't look at the financials, you are ignoring a really important piece of the big picture. If you *choose* to ignore the money, then you can skip this chapter – but *caveat emptor* (let the buyer beware).

To help you think this through, we want to show you one way to examine your college choices. One important part of strategic or "big picture" decisions in business is comparing one business opportunity to another. Various types of financial measures are used to evaluate how good an investment might be or to compare different investment possibilities to each other.

What if you started thinking about your college choice as an investment decision? Think for a minute – you and your family could spend as much money on a college education as you would spend to buy a house! Don't you think it might be wise to use some of the same logic to evaluate your college choices as you would use for other really big financial decisions?

Be warned: Some of the financials we work through in this chapter may make your head spin. Bear with us. We try to simplify this complicated process as best we can.

We know we are entering a philosophical minefield here. Discussion of *investment* in higher education relative to its *value* is a touchy subject. However, many, many college advice articles and books seem to "oversell" what you are getting from a bachelor's degree. We are simply giving you a different way of thinking about things. To help you better understand this notion of college as an investment, we have developed a tool we call the College Payback Ratio, or CPR.

Here is the basic idea: Given the size of your education investment, how long will you have to work to earn back the money you spent if you get a job in your major field of study? The CPR helps you look at the financial impact of your choices and gives you a sense of the trade-offs that go along with each choice. The CPR will allow you to examine your financial investment in the bachelor's degree relative to your degree's average market value.

Before we get into the numbers, we want to lay out a few assumptions that we have about the college decision process. You may not agree with all of these assumptions ... and that's fine. But we want you to know what is shaping our advice.

Assumption 1: University academic programs leading to a bachelor's degree are very similar across institutions. Although there are certainly differences from campus to campus and from faculty to faculty, the academic degree and program don't vary enormously from institution to institution.

Assumption 2: Bachelor's degrees vary in terms of their market value. Although your major doesn't completely determine your salary – individual talent and work ethic do come into play – there is a pretty easily identifiable salary range associated with many entry-level jobs that are commonly filled by new college graduates.

Assumption 3: All the possible value associated with higher education is not really quantifiable. The choice of a college is a uniquely personal decision. That said, you still need to examine the financial implications of the choice.

The College Payback Ratio

If you put all of these assumptions together with a few easy financial concepts, you get the College Payback Ratio (CPR). This equation consists of two pieces of financial information: 1) the **Education Investment** (EI), measured by the total price of the bachelor's degree (out-of-pocket costs) and 2) the **Marginal Market Value** (MMV) of the degree you obtain. If you put those two pieces of information together, you can figure out how many years it will take you to pay yourself back for the financial investment you make to acquire a college degree. Or think about it this way: How many dollars of education investment did you have to spend to get $1 extra in salary from having your college degree.

The equation looks like this:

$$CPR = EI/MMV$$

Some of you may be rolling your eyes. Just what are you supposed to do with this calculation? Well, we suggest you use it to look at your different college options based on the number of years it will take you to pay yourself back for each one. This will give you a way to put the choices side-by-side. The calculation will also help you to start thinking strategically about your decision by playing with either the numerator (the EI) or the denominator (the MMV). A few pages from now, we will walk you through a hypothetical analysis so you can see how to do this for yourself. But before we do, let's take a look at how we get the two pieces of information for the CPR.

Education Investment:
The Price of the College Degree

What is the size of your education investment? What is college going to cost you? You would think that these should be easy questions to answer. But part of the difficulty of the college decision is the lack of clear and easily compared information about the total price of the same degree at different colleges. If you want to buy a hamburger, it's pretty easy to compare what you get from McDonald's, Wendy's or Sonic. It gets a little harder when you start trying to compare used cars. Comparing college prices is *a lot* harder than that!

One reason that comparison is so hard is because there are so many things you need to remember to include in the total price of the degree. The price includes tuition, room and board, fees (such as for technology and recreation), books, supplies and the everyday cost of living. Though most schools have the same basic contributors to the overall bottom line, a variety of elements can affect your family's out-of-pocket expenses.

Tuition varies depending on the type of school (public or private), the location (urban, rural, Northeast, South) and reputation (selective, open access). Room and board can be influenced by on-campus residence requirements and the market for available apartments in the area. Out-of-pocket expenses might be higher or lower depending on individual eligibility for financial aid and scholarships. Financial aid is influenced by the amount of federal and state financial aid available, university endowments and tax revenue generated by the overall economy. With all these variables, it is easy to see why it's hard to nail down one clear comparable price, even when similar students apply to the same place.

To keep things simple, we are only going to look at the "real" dollars – the out-of-pocket dollars that are directly spent to get the college degree. These costs are what we call the "investment" in your college degree.

For the moment, we also aren't going to discuss financing of the college education. Think about it, you don't – or shouldn't – talk about financing a new car until after you've agreed on the price. So unless some kind of scholarship gives you a deep discount on the price, *how* you pay for college is a separate issue from the *price* you will pay for the college degree. In this chapter, we focus on the *price* of a college degree, which we call your Education Investment. We'll come back to financing options in a later chapter.

When you put it all together, your out-of-pocket investment in a college degree looks like this:

EI = Cost for ONE year of College x Years to Complete the Degree

The Market Value of Your Degree

How will having that bachelor's degree increase your annual income? To get a fair idea of this, you need to realize that, even without a college degree, you would probably still have a job. So how much more can you make *with* a college degree compared to *without* one?

According to the Census Bureau, an average person with only a high school education makes about $30,000 per year. That works out to about $15 per hour. Obviously, there are high school graduates who are millionaires, and there are people with doctorates working at McDonald's. But those are the exceptions. Generally, higher incomes correspond with higher levels of education. Therefore, you can expect that having only a high school diploma will result in lower average wages.

For our College Payback Ratio, we are interested in what we call the Marginal Market Value of your specific degree. This is how much *more* you can expect to make in one year because you have chosen to pursue education beyond high school. To get a fair comparison for decision purposes, you need to have some idea of what the average starting salary is for your major. There are several ways to go about this. One is to go to the U.S. Bureau of Labor Statistics and pull the most recent data on Occupational Employment Statistics (www.bls.gov/oes/). The OES collects information twice each year on employment and wages for more than 800 occupations. Another approach is to ask the colleges that are of interest to you what the average starting salary is for their graduates from a specific program.

To find the Marginal Market Value, simply take your major's annual starting salary and subtract the average annual pay for a worker with only a high school education. As we noted earlier, workers with only a high school education earned, on average, $30,000 a year in 2008. The difference between the two wages is the value of your particular major in the marketplace. The calculation looks like this:

MMV = Average Annual Salary for Your Major MINUS $30,000

Putting your Education Investment together with the Marginal Market Value of your degree gives you the basis for calculating your College Payback Ratio. Let's work through an example and some worksheets.

Using the CPR
Sam's Decision: Four Colleges, Four Prices

We know that this all sounds complicated – and it is. But that doesn't mean we can't take all that complexity and organize it. That is what we are going to do right now. We are going to walk a student – we'll call him "Sam" – through the CPR and see how his options stack up.

Meet Sam, a solid student – not a stellar, perfect test score, free-ride candidate but a good student who will likely perform well at college. Sam has looked around and has four very different options to consider for his college choice.

Option 1: College A is a well-respected small, private liberal-arts college that sees Sam's potential and offers him a spot within its hallowed halls. College A comes with a price tag of $27,293 for tuition and fees, which just happens to match the average cost of a private, non-profit, four-year college for 2010. Based on Sam's solid academic record, his compelling personal essay and his family's financial circumstances, College A decides to slash its advertised tuition price to $11,320 by offering Sam a scholarship. "Wow," Sam thinks to himself, "I must be smarter than I thought if the school's willing to offer me such a nice scholarship." It feels good to be that wanted, plus the campus had seemed so cozy, idyllic and, well, exclusive that day he visited.

Sam may think that discount is just for him because he's such a great guy, but that's really the average net tuition price students ended up paying at four-year private colleges for 2010-2011, according to the College Board's "Trends in College Pricing 2010" report. Before Sam jumps at the deal, he has to remember room and board, which adds on $9,700 for the school year, and books, supplies and personal expenses, which may add about $2,500. Even with the nearly 60 percent reduction in tuition costs, Sam is still looking at signing on to pay roughly $23,500 per year for the next four years or more.

Option 2: College B is a four-year public university that is nationally known for research, but it is in another state.

Strategy Tip

Depending on your family's income, you can get a tax deduction for tuition and fees. Married couples making less than $160,000 can deduct up to $4,000 from their adjusted gross income. For most families, this translates into about a $1,000 tax rebate. But this ONLY applies to tuition and required fees and supplies. Room and board and non-required books are not eligible for the tax deduction. Here's another thing you need to know about scholarships and taxes: If you are lucky enough to get money for room and board, the government considers that taxable income.

It has a good reputation, a large selection of programs and a *great* basketball team. Sure, the campus seemed a bit big and overwhelming (it has 20,000 undergraduate students), but everyone Sam talked to during the campus visit seemed so darn friendly. Plus, everywhere he looked, students were wearing their blue and white school colors. It was even sunny that day, and the campus tour showed off the highlights of the new recreation center and the stadium. For out-of-state students, College B comes with a sticker price of $19,595, which just happens to equal the average out-of-state tuition and fees for four-year public colleges nationwide in 2010. Based on the information submitted in Sam's financial aid form, the school offers him the discounted tuition price of $13,000, which approximates the average net tuition cost for out-of-state public four-year universities. Sam again must remember the $8,535 in room and board costs and the $2,500 for books, personal expenses and travel. That puts the cost of attending Sam's out-of-state option at about $24,000 or more per year for the next four to six years.

Wait a minute, Sam is probably thinking, that's actually slightly more expensive than the smaller, more exclusive private school. Perhaps those college coaches and admissions counselors really are right to insist that private colleges often end up costing roughly the same as public institutions in terms of net cost. And since the costs are relatively equal, then those advice books that say the college decision should really be about personal choice and fit must be right after all.

Not so fast. Let's look at the offer from College C.

Option 3: College C is also a nationally recognized research university, but it is in Sam's home state. It scores well in the various college rankings but has a sad sack sports history. The few times that its teams have actually been picked to win, they invented new ways to lose. The university is big, even bigger than the out-of-state school Sam visited (there are 25,000 undergraduate students). Plus, it rained the entire day he was there. It was a nice campus, sure, and everyone seemed perfectly pleasant and helpful, but compared to those other two schools, this one just didn't excite Sam's interest. It could be simply that the "grass is always greener" farther away from home, but those other two schools seemed so much more *collegiate.*

Sam himself had pretty much ruled out College C based on the impression he got during the campus visit. His mother liked it; his dad did too, although Dad kept muttering that the school should fire its athletic director. Sam probably wouldn't have even bothered to look at College C's financial offer if his parents hadn't insisted.

Strategy Tip

A grant is an award from the government that is based on financial need and often comes from state or federal governments. A scholarship is an award from a college or other organization that may or may not be based on financial need. You do not have to pay back a grant or a scholarship. One sales pitch that some, more expensive, colleges make is that the high price of the college will make you eligible for government grants to help cover the price. This is often true because of the very strange way that grant awards are calculated. HOWEVER, the government grant alone will NEVER be enough to cover the majority of the tuition price tag at expensive schools.

The sticker price for tuition at College C is $7,605, which just happens to coincide with the average published cost for tuition and fees at public four-year schools nationwide in 2010. Grants, scholarships and tax benefits reduce the net cost to $1,540, which just happens to match the average net in-state tuition cost at four-year public schools for 2010-2011. When he adds in room and board – $8,540 – books and expenses, Sam is likely facing about $12,500 per year for the next four to six years. Huh, Sam thinks to himself, that's about half the cost of the other two schools. Dad thinks, "Wow! Please go with the cheaper one," but, being a supportive dad, he keeps those thoughts to himself.

Option 4: College D is a regional university about 30 miles away from Sam's hometown. Sam only agreed to look at it because his father went there and his mother likes the idea of Sam being close to home. Because this university wants to attract strong students, Sam's grades are good enough to qualify for the full-tuition scholarship – worth $6,000 – offered to in-state students. The campus is noticeably smaller and a bit more outdated than the two other public universities Sam visited, and its six-year graduation rate of 41.3 percent is much lower than that of the other three schools. The school offers the typical general education courses and surprisingly just opened a state-of-the-art space center laboratory, which would allow Sam to get hands-on experience pursuing his love of aeronautics. The university also has a strong music program, which is his second choice of study. (Yes, the minds of students really are that fascinating.) Room and board is lower than average at $6,192. Add in books and supplies, and the total cost to attend is under $7,700 per year. Or, in other words, he can earn his bachelor's degree for about $38,000, even if it takes him five years to finish.

The first step for Sam and his family is to calculate the price tag for each of his four college options. Using our worksheet (see Chapter 14 for a blank copy for your own calculations), here is what Sam and his family would put together. This exercise would not only allow them to compare the basic out-of-pocket costs associated with each university option, but it would also give them the Education Investment numbers needed to calculate Sam's CPR for each choice.

Calculating Sam's Education Investment				
	College A	College B	College C	College D
A. Total Stated Price				
1. Tuition & Fees	$27,293	$19,595	$7,605	$6,000
2. Room & Board	$9,700	$8,535	$8,540	$6,192
3. Books & Supplies	$2,500	$2,500	$2,500	$2,500
B. Rebates				
1. Scholarships & Grants	$14,973	$5,595	$5,065	$6,000
2. Tax Deduction	$1,000	$1,000	$1,000	$1,000
C. Education Investment Per Year (A-B)	$23,520	$24,035	$12,580	$7,692
D. 4 -Year Education Investment (Line C x 4)	**$94,080**	**$96,140**	**$50,320**	**$30,768**
E. 5 -Year Education Investment (Line C x 5)	**$117,600**	**$120,175**	**$62,900**	**$38,460**
F. 6 -Year Education Investment (Line C x 6)	**$141,120**	**$144,210**	**$75,480**	**$46,152**

Finding Sam's MMV

Let's assume that the career Sam plans to pursue is likely to pay, on average, $47,000 per year. This is roughly equal to the 2008 median wage for full-time workers between the ages of 25 and 35 who have a bachelor's degree, according to U.S. Census data. Because we want to examine the value of the bachelor's degree itself, we also need to take into account how much Sam might make without the degree – if he had decided to get a job instead. That means we need to subtract the $30,000 annual income that he could expect to make if he had skipped college and gone straight to work. What's left over (in this case, $17,000) is the MMV for Sam's college major.

Calculating the Marginal Market Value of Sam's Future Degree	
A. Annual Market Value of an Entry-Level Job in Sam's Future Field (median)	$47,000
B. Annual Market Value of a Job Requiring Only a High School Diploma (median)	$30,000
C. Marginal Market Value of Job (per year) (A minus B)	$17,000

Calculating the CPR

So what kind of financial return can Sam expect from his college choice? We have already figured the total out-of-pocket costs he and his parents can expect to pay. Using the CPR, Sam can compare the "payback period" for each of his college options. To do that, he would need to divide the total cost for obtaining his degree by the extra $17,000 he might expect to earn each year because of that degree. The following worksheet shows what the payback period would likely be for each of Sam's college choices depending on how long it takes him to graduate. As you can clearly see, higher costs tend to require longer payback periods.

When businesses use such a method to make decisions about how to invest money in various projects, the rule of thumb is that investments with shorter payback periods rank higher than those with longer ones. The idea is that investments with shorter payback periods are less risky; thus, they are more likely to result in a good bang for the buck invested. Also, with any investment, there are *lots* of variables that are increasingly uncertain the longer you look out into the future. A shorter payback period means there is less of a chance that the economy, the job market or your (or your parents') life situation might change. (Just think of

Calculating Sam's College Payback Ratio				
	College A	College B	College C	College D
A. 4-Year Education Investment	$94,080	$96,140	$50,320	$30,768
B. 5-Year Education Investment	$117,600	$120,175	$62,900	$38,460
C. 6-Year Education Investment	$141,120	$144,210	$75,480	$46,152
D . Marginal Market Value of Job	$17,000	$17,000	$17,000	$17,000
Number of Years Before Sam's Investment Is Repaid				
E. CPR - 4 Years to Degree (A divided by D)	5.53	5.66	2.96	1.81
F. CPR - 5 Years to Degree (B divided by D)	6.92	7.07	3.70	2.26
G. CPR - 6 Years to Degree (C divided by D)	8.30	8.48	4.44	2.71

all those students who enrolled as freshmen in 2005 and graduated in 2009 or 2010 facing an unemployment rate that topped 11 percent among young people!)

Playing "What If"

If you look at the college choice purely as a business decision, then Sam and his parents should be looking at College C or College D. If Sam picks College C, then he needs to work hard to make sure that he finishes in four years. That means staying focused on his major, staying on track in his classes and taking no extra time for a study abroad or other experiential program unless it fits with his major. If Sam picks College D, he and his family might have more flexibility for more "exploratory" options.

But that's a detached, what's-good-for-you kind of view, about as exciting as eating bran and brussel sprouts when you really want chocolate. What if, in Sam's mind, a nearly six-year payback period doesn't seem so bad? After all, he really liked College A, and he thinks he can convince his parents that the higher price and longer payback period are worth it because of the wonderful educational experiences he expects to have. That's a legitimate decision, and Sam and his family could make that choice. Plenty of students have. Sam's parents may decide to go along with College A because they figure that Sam will ultimately do better in the job market with a degree from the more prestigious school and that his potentially higher earning power, in turn, will make the payback quicker than our estimate.

OK, let's play "what if?" But instead of painting a rosy outcome, which students and parents invariably do, let's think about a different scenario. What if instead of landing a job out of school paying $47,000 a year, Sam ends up in one of the many jobs that pay less than $35,000? (About 25 percent of people between the ages of 25 and 35 with bachelor's degrees make less than $35,000 per year.) What if, during his coursework, Sam discovers a passion for helping people and lands a job as a mental health case manager, paying about $32,000 a year? The job is emotionally rewarding but not nearly as financially rewarding as he had expected when he headed off to school planning to study aeronautics. At $32,000, his annual earnings are only about $2,000 more than the average salary for workers with only a high school diploma. Let's see what happens to his CPR in this scenario.

With an MMV of only $2,000, it will take 47 years for Sam's earnings to cover the cost of the investment he made to attend College A. Even if Sam chooses College D, it will take 15 years for him to earn enough to cover what he and his family spent on his schooling.

The point of this exercise is not to discourage anyone from pursuing college or even pursuing an expensive college option. The point is to make you understand the

Calculating Sam's College Payback Ratio If His Job Is Lower Wage				
	College A	College B	College C	College D
A. 4-Year Education Investment	$94,080	$96,140	$50,320	$30,768
B. 5-Year Education Investment	$117,600	$120,175	$62,900	$38,460
C. 6-Year Education Investment	$141,120	$144,210	$75,480	$46,152
D . Marginal Market Value of Job	$2,000	$2,000	$2,000	$2,000
Number of Years Before Sam's Investment Is Repaid				
E. CPR - 4 Years to Degree (A divided by D)	47.04	48.07	25.16	15.38
F. CPR - 5 Years to Degree (B divided by D)	58.80	60.09	31.45	19.23
G. CPR - 6 Years to Degree (C divided by D)	70.56	72.11	37.74	23.08

importance of choosing wisely. Our goal is to give you a different, more dollars and cents (and sense), perspective about how to make that college degree worth your investment of time and money. Yes, these are simplified, rule-of-thumb calculations that don't take into account all the potential value of a college experience or the range of economic power you may create. Increasingly, your education and skill level are critical for landing a job, nearly any job, in the 21st century American economy.

The stakes are high and getting even higher. If you truly want to make education "pay," you need to make smart, strategic choices. And for all the Sams and Samanthas out there who have their hearts set on a college that really doesn't fit their family circumstances, they may get an early start on learning the biggest lesson of adulthood: You can't always get what you want. But with some good planning and smart choices, you just might find, as the old song says, "you get what you need."

Cram Session

- The choice you make today about where to go to college can have long-, long-term effects on your economic and personal well-being.
- The College Payback Ratio estimates how long it will take to recover your education investment.
- The major you pick can have a big impact on your CPR.
- A shorter payback period for your college investment is usually preferable to a longer payback period.

Key Concepts:
Advanced Placement & CLEP
co-operative education
strategic planning

Chapter 4
Reduce the CPR: Strategies for Minimizing Your Investment

Often, families think that the only way to lower the out-of-pocket price of a college degree (the EI) is to get a scholarship or a government grant. It's true that these types of awards can make a huge difference in the overall price of a bachelor's degree. But here are a few reality checks: First, only a relatively small percentage of traditional age students are eligible for government grants. The second reality check is that only a very small percentage of students get a big enough scholarship or grant to cover the entire out-of-pocket price of a four-year college degree. Finally, a lot of scholarships and grants come with strings attached. For grants, the biggest strings are that you have to maintain a minimum grade-point average and complete a minimum number of credit hours to remain eligible. For federal Pell Grants, your family income must be below a designated level. For scholarships, the GPA requirements may be much higher than for grants, they may be attached to a particular major, or they may only be guaranteed for one year. So, if you don't want to rely on scholarships and grants to lower your out-of-pocket price, what are some other strategies that might work?

Price Reduction Strategies Everyone Can Try

In the last chapter, we explored the potentially huge cost differences between colleges and showed that in-state public institutions, particularly smaller, regional ones, tend to offer the best bang for the buck. But if you want to expand your college options, there are strategies for lowering your education investment and reducing the payback period.

EI Strategy 1: Start accumulating college credits *before* **you get there!**

Shaving a year off the traditional four-year program could have a dramatic impact on the CPR. One less year spent on education and one less year forgoing earnings would dramatically improve the odds that your investment will pay off. You can start to lower the costs of earning a bachelor's degree even before you set foot on campus. College-bound students at high schools across the country are taking Advanced Placement classes in everything from world history and Chinese to statistics and computer science. Students who complete the AP coursework can spend $86 to take a test in each subject; students with demonstrated financial need can even have that cost reduced. Students who achieve a certain score may be able to have their coursework count as college credit.

Not all colleges give the credit, but in many cases, students can bypass several freshman general education classes by using AP credit. College Board, which administers AP tests, reports that 90 percent of colleges accept AP classes, but it stresses that the decision to grant credit and placement is up to the individual schools. In other words, *caveat emptor* – buyer beware. You'll need to check with each college you're considering to find out which ones have generous policies regarding AP classes and which don't.

Many college-bound students, especially those coming out of competitive, largely affluent high schools, take AP classes because they think that's what they need to do to get accepted into their elite college of choice. These students think of AP classes as a "market signal" that they are serious students, but many don't bother to take the test that gives them the college credit. (You have to do both if you are going to reduce your out-of-pocket price.)

Even worse, they often don't even try to use the credit at their chosen college or university. Their faulty logic usually goes something like this: "Well, if I take the same class at college, I won't have to work very hard to get a decent grade, and that will mean more time to party!" Yet, in their efforts to line up easy A's their freshman year, they fail to understand one college reality: If you are able to keep up and excel in AP classes during high school, the odds are pretty good that you are ready for sophomore-level work at all but the most demanding and elite universities.

CLEP, the College-Level Examination Program, is another way potentially to "test out" of low-level college courses. Some colleges have generous policies for giving course credit for scoring well on CLEP tests. Other schools don't accept them at all. You will need to check with the schools you're considering to determine whether this may be an option

Reality Check

If your high school offers AP classes but you haven't taken any, two reasons might explain your reluctance: If the reason you aren't doing AP is that you just don't want to do the extra work, well, think about it. You are going to have to do that level of work in college, so if you aren't willing to do it now, what would make you think you will be ready a year or two from now? Don't waste your money (or your parents' money) if you aren't really ready to go to college and do college-level work. Consider taking a "gap year" to WORK, SAVE MONEY and decide what you want to do with your life.

The second reason that you might not be going for the AP classes is that you just aren't academically ready to take them. If that's the case, then you need to think about starting college at a place where you can handle the workload and that has support services if you run into academic trouble.

for you. The fee to take each subject test is comparable to the cost for AP tests, but you may need to purchase study materials in order to perform well on the test. If the school of your choice has a generous policy regarding CLEP tests, this may be an economical way to skip a semester or two ahead. However, if you don't score high enough, you will have wasted your money. If CLEP is an option at your school of choice, it probably is worth the cost to try to test out of as many of your freshman courses as you can.

For More Information

To learn about CLEP, visit: www.collegeboard.com/student/ testing/clep/exams.html

To learn about AP exams, visit: www.collegeboard.com/student/ testing/ap/about.html

Some states, such as Minnesota, Ohio and Iowa, offer an even better deal through a program called Postsecondary Enrollment Options. PSEO is an example of dual-enrollment programs, which are great opportunities to reduce the cost of college. PSEO programs allow academically qualified high school students (usually juniors and seniors) to enroll in college courses and receive both high school and college credit for the work. Better yet, the cost of the classes and books is paid for by the state or local school district. In 2008, Ohio launched the Seniors to Sophomores program to encourage high school students to enroll and effectively skip their freshman year of college – for free.

School districts in other states are starting "Middle College," where small public high schools are set up on college campuses. During their junior and senior years of high school, students are able to take college freshman and sophomore classes along with the college students and without having to pay anything extra.

College policies vary on whether and how they allow these courses to transfer for credit, but these options are ways to reduce the amount of time you have to spend on your bachelor's degree.

EI Strategy 2: Make the most of your time when you get to campus. Max out your course load.

Another way to cut the number of years you and your family pay for college is to maximize your personal productivity on campus. Before you make your college choice, check into the school's policy regarding class load. A typical load for an undergraduate semester is 15 credit hours. Averaging that number of credit hours per semester will usually be enough to get you out of college in four years, provided that you haven't been set back by switching majors or failing a course or two.

Typically, colleges and universities charge a flat "full-time" rate, whether you take 12 credit hours or 18. Too many 12-credit semesters are among the traps that stretch out students' time in school. Falling below 12 credit hours may jeopardize any grants or scholarships you receive and maybe even student housing. However, if you can handle the heavier course load, you can pick up credits (or catch up if you have fallen behind) by adding an extra class periodically. Try it first by using some "free" (and not-too-demanding) electives, which in most programs can be anything from basket weaving to hip hop.

If it looks as though the added class is going to be too much to handle and might have a negative impact on your grades in more important classes, you can always withdraw. The only cost beyond what you're already paying would be the price of textbooks – which, we admit, can be a hefty sum. But if you can handle 18 credit hours per semester instead of the typical 15, you can reduce your time in school by at least a full semester (half of a year).

EI Strategy 3: Have a productive summer!

If you go away from home to attend school, look into taking a class or two at your local community college during your summer break. Community college classes are significantly cheaper than classes at four-year schools, plus room and board at home with your parents is "free."

(Or, if your parents do charge you rent, we assume it's a pittance compared to what you get in return.) At $70 or $80 per credit hour, you could pick up a class for under $250. For basic general education classes for freshmen or sophomores or for those electives that are necessary for reaching your total credit hour requirement, community college is a good deal.

Strategy Tip

When on your trip to check out campuses, you want to ask about any "articulation" agreements. An articulation agreement means that two universities have a contract to accept each other's classes. This will reduce your paperwork if you are trying to get credits to transfer.

Just make sure that your college will transfer the credit to your degree program before you pay your money. At many colleges and universities, this means filling out some paperwork and getting a few signatures before you take the classes. Don't neglect the paperwork! You want to make sure that everything will transfer to your university with no surprises.

The other thing about transfer credit is that it often doesn't affect your GPA because the credit, not the grade, is what transfers in. Strategic use of transfer credit can have the added impact of protecting your GPA.

This same strategy works even if your regular campus is one of those expensive private colleges. If you go home for the summer, you can take a few courses at your local public university. You can do this in the classroom or even online. By taking advantage of online offerings from an institute, college or university, you can sometimes have a summer job and knock out three to six credit hours for your collegiate program at the same time. Again, just make sure *ahead of time* that the courses will transfer to your home campus.

EI Strategy 4: Go for a paycheck and a grade.

Co-operative learning programs represent another opportunity for making college more affordable. They don't reduce the cost; in fact, co-op programs may extend your course of study by a year or more. However, co-op programs, particularly those that have been around for a while, tend to place students in good-paying jobs. Participating students may alternate between a semester in class and a semester on the job. Or, in other models, students may spend part of their day in class and part of their day on the job. Engineering, science and business fields lend themselves to co-op experiences, but the model can work in other fields and has been garnering new interest as schools have begun to embrace experiential learning. It's not uncommon for co-op students to earn enough to cover a substantial portion of their school costs. In addition, they have the opportunity to apply what they are learning in the classroom, gain valuable on-the-job skills and make important contacts in the work world. It's one example of how students can add value to their college education.

Strategic Sam and His College Options

Let's go back to Sam's choice. Sam really wanted to go to small, private College A. He had fallen in love with the campus and really felt at home there. Fortunately, Sam and his family worked out a plan for college that included a combination of high school AP credits, 18 hours of transfer credit from the regional university close to home (six hours each summer), and a one semester co-op experience. Because Sam knew that his choice of College A really put a burden on his family's finances, he decided that taking 18 hours for some semesters was his way of showing his family that he really appreciated the opportunity.

This admittedly "best-case" strategy has some pretty dramatic results. Sam would be able to cut the CPR for College A to a little over three years and reduce the out-

EI Strategies Could Result in Big Savings for Sam

A. Total Stated Price for College A

1. Tuition & Fees	$27,293
2. Room & Board	$9,700
3. Books & Supplies	$2,500

B. Rebate

1. Scholarships & Grants	$14,973
2. Tax Deduction	$1,000

C. Education Investment Per Year (A minus B) — $23,520

D. Effective Price Per Credit Hour (Line C/30) — $784
(One-fourth of 120-credit hour program)

E. 4-Year Education Investment (Line D x 4) — **$94,080**

F. Education Investment Strategies

1. Credit for 9 hours of high school AP classes	$7,056
2. Transfer of 18 credits	$14,112
3. Earnings from one semester co-op	$4,000
4. Savings from taking 18 hours/semester	$11,760

G. TOTAL Adjusted Education Investment (E minus F) — **$57,152**

Percent Saved — **39%**

Savings From EI Strategies Would Cut Sam's CPR

H. TOTAL Adjusted Education Investment	$57,152
I. Marginal Market Value of Sam's Future Degree	$17,000
J. College Payback Ratio in years (H divided by I)	**3.36**

of-pocket cost by *39 percent*. By effectively applying all the strategies we laid out earlier (and having a cooperative College A adviser and student services personnel), Sam and his family would be able to bring the cost down to a range that better fit their family finances.

Other Approaches to Reducing the Price of a College Education

EI Strategy 5: Start close to home.

One very cost-effective way to attend college that is often ignored is to start your four-year degree at a local community college or junior college. The average published tuition price for attending a two-year public institution full time was less than $2,600 in 2009-2010. Full-time students attending community college received $3,000, on average, in grant aid and tax benefits. That is enough to cover tuition and fees and put nearly $500 toward books. Scholarships may also be available to reward academic merit and support students of particular backgrounds or those pursuing specific fields of interest.

Remember, one of our assumptions is that a lot of college courses, particularly those that are called "general education," are very similar, regardless of whether they are taught at an elite private college, a four-year public university, online or even at a community or junior college. If you knew much about how universities and community colleges staff their freshman and sophomore courses, you would know that the professor you might have for Freshman English at the Namebrand University could be the same instructor for Freshman English at the community college down the road. Often, professors who teach general education and entry-level major courses are untenured and earn their living by contracting to teach at more than one institution at the same time.

Living at home and attending community college for two years while you work through the general education requirements you'll need for most fields of study would cut at least $20,000 off the cost of tuition, room and board at many four-year public institutions. Yes, it means you'll be at home with your family for two extra years; you'll delay the fun, excitement and self-discovery of being on your own, but that $20,000 savings is huge. You'll have plenty of time ahead of you to be out on your own, and, given the number of unemployed, underemployed or debt-laden college graduates who are moving back in with their parents, you may find that your financial savvy puts you ahead of the game. Think about it this way, you can earn a bachelor's degree for potentially half the price and still graduate with the name of the four-year college of your choice on your degree. It's a win-win.

Just be careful to ensure ahead of time that the courses you take at the local community college will transfer to your four-year school of choice *and* will apply toward your degree. You want to make sure that you get full credit for all of your work. Students who transfer from one school to another sometimes have difficulty getting all their credits to count. Whenever that happens, it's money and time down the drain. Do your homework and make a four-year plan of study, even if your plan has you starting at a two-year school.

EI Strategy 6: Forget four years and just go for two.

Among its predicted 20 fastest-growing jobs for 2006-2016, the federal government's Occupational Outlook Handbook (OOH) listed nine that require only a two-year associate's degree. Fields that the OOH expected to experience the largest percentage growth are: veterinary technologists and technicians, physical therapist assistants, environmental science and protection technicians, and cardiovascular technologists and technicians. Areas that are likely to see the largest increase in the number of jobs are: registered nurses, computer support specialists, paralegal and legal assistants, and legal secretaries.

A two-year associate's degree, which you can complete either at a public community college or at a private vocational or technical school, can be a bargain. Not only do you save at least two years of tuition costs, you also will be out in the workforce armed with marketable skills two years earlier. That means instead of paying for two more years of education, you'll be getting paid and getting job experience.

Note that we used the term "marketable skills." That's because community colleges and two-year technical or medical programs tend to be much more responsive to the needs of the markets they serve. Community colleges are designed to do what their name implies: They strive to serve the needs of their communities, both educational needs and business needs. If community college officials learn that a particularly important skill seems scarce, they are much more likely than their four-year counterparts to add coursework, or even develop certificate or degree programs, in those key areas.

For example, Hocking College in Nelsonville, Ohio, saw the rise in popularity for hybrid vehicles and recognized that there was a shortage of mechanics with the skills needed to maintain and work on these new engines. In response, the two-year school, which has a knack for hands-on learning, created an automotive hybrids major as part of its associate's degree program in alternative energy and fuel cells. Students who complete the automotive hybrids course of study can put their knowledge to work as a fleet, automotive service or vehicular laboratory technician or as a salesperson for diagnostic equipment.

Working on cars today is much more high-tech than a generation, or even a decade, ago. Cars today come equipped with dozens of microprocessors, making it difficult for owners to pop the hood and do maintenance work themselves. For this reason, along with the fact that many skilled automotive mechanics are reaching retirement age, the 2010-2011 Occupational Outlook Handbook predicts job opportunities for automotive technicians to be good, estimating 5 percent growth in employment through 2018. The OOH predicts that workers with postsecondary training and certification and those with specialized knowledge, such as in hybrid-fuel technology, will be particularly in demand. Median salary is about $35,100 annually. However, technicians certified in high-demand skills can command higher salaries. The National Automotive Technicians Education Foundation cites a demand for technicians nationwide and estimates annual salaries of $60,000 or more.

At a cost of about $2,500 in tuition and fees for a year of full-time study, the Hocking College program is a bargain – and may be a wise investment if you think you might enjoy a career working on cars. Hocking College offers other interesting two-year, hands-on programs, including: digital game design, ecotourism and adventure travel, baking, parks and recreation, spa management, construction management, farrier science and wilderness horsemanship. Now that sounds nothing like high school, right?

Belmont Technical College in Belmont, Ohio, is recognized as a national leader in providing hands-on training in historic restoration skills through its two-year program in building preservation technology. The program has been around for more than 20 years and draws students from all over the country. Cost for 15 credit hours per semester, which would typically equal a full-time load, is about $2,500 per year. The Occupational Outlook Handbook predicts job opportunities for contractors with restoration skills to be good through 2018. Median salary for brickmasons, for example, was nearly $47,000 in 2009, but top earners made $77,000 or more.

A quick disclaimer: We are by no means pushing Ohio schools. We just tend to be more familiar with their offerings. There are interesting programs at two-year schools in every state. If you really can't stomach the thought of four more years of school after high school, you owe it to yourself to check them out.

EI Strategy 7: Make sure you *need* four years for your career goal.

In the past several years, many colleges and universities have expanded programs that provide training and take a vocational view of higher education. Because of this expansion of the workforce development mission, particularly in public universities, the gap between degrees offered at universities versus community colleges has narrowed. Some fields rely on licensure. Preparing for these career paths may be done through either a two-year or a four-year program. One way to save money is by choosing the two-year track, which is typically offered by a community college or technical school, instead of pursuing a traditional bachelor's degree.

Here's just one example to illustrate our point: If the idea of scraping and flossing other people's teeth doesn't make you want to run the other way, you may want to look into the high-growth field of dental hygiene. The most recent Occupational Outlook Handbook, updating job forecasts through 2018, lists dental hygienists among the fastest-growing occupations, with an expected 36 percent increase in workers.

Dental hygienists earned, on average, more than $32 an hour in 2009, meaning their annual full-time salaries topped $64,000. Although some dental hygienists earn a bachelor's degree, completing an associate's program – and passing licensure requirements – is all that is necessary for an entry-level job, which tends to pay about $25 to $30 an hour.

Choosing to pursue a four-year degree in a field in which an associate's degree is enough is not necessarily a bad choice. The idea behind those general education requirements is that they make you a more "well-rounded" person. It's good to have a broad base of knowledge in life, even if the career you choose is specifically technical. A bachelor's degree also means you will be able to go on to pursue a master's degree later if you want to open new doors of opportunity. Plus, as we've said before, it's fun to be in college. But it's also fun actually to be making money and buying stuff that you want.

It's not wrong to take a different path to the same career, even if it's longer and more costly. But you owe it to yourself and your parents to understand the true costs and opportunities so that you can make an informed choice.

Cram Session

- Look into ways to get college credit before even going to college.

- One very cost-effective way to attend college that is too often ignored is to start your four-year degree at a local community college or junior college. The average cost for attending a two-year public institution full time in 2010-2011 was $2,713.

- A two-year associate's degree, which you can complete either at a public community college or at a private vocational or technical school, may be a bargain. Not only do you save at least two years of tuition costs, you also can be out in the workforce earning a salary two years earlier.

Key Concepts:
professional development
supply and demand
marketable knowledge
Marginal Market Value

Chapter 5
Strategies for Maximizing the Market Value of Your Degree

In the movie *Groundhog Day,* Bill Murray's obnoxious character, Phil, can't help but scoff when he learns that the object of his desire, Rita (played by Andie MacDowell), spent her time in college studying 19th century French poetry.

"What a waste of time!" he snorts, before he learns yet another lesson from that endlessly looping day: You shouldn't belittle other people's passions, especially if you want them to like you. Phil tries to soft-pedal his scorn by calling Rita's college major choice a sign of an incredibly strong and bold person.

But another lesson of that recurring scene is that Phil's initial instinct, while impolite, might be right: Are you kidding? You thought you could find a job with that?

Rita's *paying* job, after all, was to produce Phil's weather segments, not write, interpret or simply enjoy the beauty and depth of long-dead French poets.

That 1993 movie (yes, we realize that was around the time you were born; think of it as an oldie but a goodie) was illuminating in ways beyond its mystical Zen storyline that had Phil reliving the same day over and over and over until he finally became a better person. The film also inadvertently tells us something about the changing nature of a college education. *In a knowledge economy, some kinds of knowledge have more market value than other kinds of knowledge.*

That's a fact. Actually, it always has been a fact of life of capitalism. Doctors (one type of knowledge) have tended to earn more than nurses (different type of knowledge). Engineers (one type of knowledge) have tended to earn more than assembly workers (different type of knowledge). Professors (one type of knowledge) have tended to earn more than preschool teachers (different type of knowledge).

A college education today is different than it was decades ago. Because more and more employers are requiring bachelor's degrees among entry-level workers, college has become more directly tied to employment. That's partly because many jobs have become more technologically complex. But it's also partly because employers consider a college degree to be a great screening tool. The fact that you have earned a degree tells them a little something about not only your aptitude but your perseverance. Whether you really need that particular degree for that particular job is another matter.

Many people in higher education, especially those with a more liberal-arts leaning, don't like to admit this, but the business of college, especially for the traditional 18-to-22 age group, is now largely about *professional development.* The pursuit of a bachelor's degree for the vast majority of students heading off to college each year is about getting a job. Plain and simple. Yet, the structure of college is still geared around *personal development.* That's why you will still face all those general education requirements of philosophy, foreign language and history even though you plan to be an engineer or a computer programmer. That's also why you'll still have the option of pursuing your passion for comparative French literature and art history even though the prospects of your landing a job in either of those fields are pretty slim.

Our point here is not to suggest that having a passion for French poetry or art history is bad. It's merely to point out that there's a difference between knowledge and *marketable* knowledge. A knowledge e*conomy* doesn't reward all knowledge; it rewards marketable knowledge, or knowledge that someone (an employer) is willing to pay for.

You're not the only one struggling to make a good decision about your field of study. Colleges are struggling with this themselves. They have long experienced a tension between their personal development mission (think of the intellectual and moral growth that humanities classes encourage) and their professional development role (think of the skills acquisition that occurs in fields such as business and medicine). Yet, over the past decade or so, a clear winner in this academic tug-of-war has emerged: professional development. The overwhelming majority of students go to college today because that's their most likely path to a decent-paying job.

The more the knowledge economy values your major, the bigger the spread between the salary you will earn with a bachelor's degree and the salary you might have earned without one. The higher the Marginal Market Value of your degree, the quicker your education investment will be repaid. So what are some stategies for increasing the odds that you have a degree with higher market value in the knowledge economy?

MMV Strategy 1: Understand the implications of supply and demand.

Supply and demand is a fundamental concept in economics. If you want to approach the college decision in a more business-like way and treat it like the significant financial investment it is, you need to understand the implications of supply and demand. Why is it that most undergraduates who major in accounting make so much

Reality Check

What does all this discussion of the changing marketplace and the changing college mission mean to you? Well, it means that it's up to you to choose your field of study wisely and with a realistic view of the end goal. You need to focus on acquiring skills that will help you get a job after graduation. This doesn't mean you can't pursue your passions for fields that are not as highly valued or as highly demanded in the knowledge economy, but it does mean you will need to think about ways to make your passions marketable or minimize your investment — or both. You don't want to make the same mistake that far too many students do of spending a lot to acquire knowledge that is little rewarded. That's how we end up with well-educated English majors working as Starbucks baristas and drowning in debt.

more money than equally talented students who major in history? Whether you think it's fair or not, that's the powerful force of supply and demand at work.

Differences in the market value for knowledge are based on two things: 1) the value of the knowledge itself and 2) how much of the knowledge is needed in the current economy. Let's assume for the moment that all knowledge has value (No. 1). If that's the case, then what must make a big difference in the knowledge economy is No. 2.

To illustrate this, let's think about a particular field. The knowledge economy has some demand for people who specialize in, say, Ancient Middle Eastern Art. It's a small demand, but, as we noted earlier, all knowledge has some degree of value. The problem arises when there are more Ancient Middle Eastern Art majors than there is demand in the economy. When that happens, the market value of the degree is going to be lower. That's because a lot of people are competing for just a few jobs.

This is why some degrees in some knowledge areas are always going to pay more than others. Those fields with higher pay tend to have fewer workers with the right match of in-demand skills. In the marketplace today, we tend to have more history and psychology majors than we have jobs for people with those particular sets of knowledge. That's why history professors tend to make less money than economics professors and why a large number of psychology majors work as office managers and customer service representatives.

That's the economic reality you need to understand and operate within, but that reality does not need to keep you from pursuing your passions and your dreams. If you have a burning desire to study a field that is not in high demand in the knowledge economy, go ahead. But you owe it to yourself to think about ways to make your passions more marketable or pursue strategies to minimize your education investment – or both. You don't want to make the mistake that far too many students do: Assuming that whatever field they study, they will be amply rewarded. That kind of thinking drives far too many students to invest a lot of money and time to acquire knowledge that brings them little financial return in the marketplace.

MMV Strategy 2: Compare the market value for different college degrees.

PayScale.com, the online salary survey site, has compiled lists of the top occupations for workers holding bachelor's degrees in various fields. Although the survey has shortcomings, these lists should give you some idea of how the market values the degree you think you want to pursue.

To examine the market value of a particular degree, you need some useful pieces of information:

1) The number of overall degrees awarded in your field each year (Supply).

2) The absolute number of future jobs available in a

particular knowledge area (Demand).

3) The projected growth rate for this type of job in the future (Demand).

4) The average pay associated with this type of job.

The following table shows the top 10 bachelor's degrees awarded in recent years. As you can see, the most common by far was a bachelor's degree in some area of business, with 335,254 bachelor's degrees conferred in 2007-2008 alone! Beyond students with a passion for business, the field is a common choice among students who haven't figured out their career path. That represents a relatively safe, reasonable choice, given that the Occupational Outlook Handbook for 2010-2011 predicts a need for 178,000 more management analysts by 2018. That's a 24 percent increase over the 747,000 workers employed in the field in 2008. Median pay for management analysts was about $75,000 in May 2009, according to the Bureau of Labor Statistics. The OOH also predicts a need for nearly 280,000 more accountants and auditors by 2018. Accountants and auditors had a median annual salary of about $60,000 in May 2009.

Here is why it is important to look at both supply *and* demand: More than 167,000 bachelor's degrees

Top 10 Bachelor's Degrees Conferred		
Field of Study	2006-2007	2007-2008
Business	327,531	335,254
Social Sciences & History	164,183	167,363
Health Professions & Related Clinical Sciences	101,810	111,478
Education	105,641	102,582
Psychology	90,039	92,587
Visual & Performing Arts	85,186	87,703
Biological & Biomedical Sciences	75,151	77,854
Communication & Journalism	74,783	76,382
Engineering	67,092	68,676
English	55,122	55,038

Source: National Center for Education Statistics

were conferred in 2007-2008 in social science areas, such as sociology, political science and history. Many students in these areas hope to go on to graduate school or plan to pursue a professional degree, such as law. It's worth pointing out that only about 43,000 law degrees are conferred annually, and there are far fewer doctorate degrees in these areas. That means, regardless of their original intent, most of these young graduates likely *will not* pursue schooling beyond their bachelor's degree. Nearly 93,000 students graduated with a bachelor's degree in psychology in 2007-2008. Given that only about 21,000 students earned a master's degree in psychology in 2007-2008 and little more than 5,000 earned a doctorate, it's safe to assume that the vast majority of those who graduated with a bachelor's degree in psychology pursued no further education in that field. (Of course, some of them may have decided to pursue a graduate degree in another field, such as earning a Master of Business Administration.)

So what kinds of jobs do people who hold bachelor's degrees in these fields actually have and what can they expect to earn? According to PayScale.com's survey, among the 10 jobs *most often held* by workers with a bachelor's degree in psychology, six had median annual salaries below $40,000. Mental health case managers had the lowest pay, at $32,600. Human resource managers, at $69,300, and employment recruiters, at $71,700, were the top-paying positions listed. For some of the jobs – administrative assistant, customer service representative and office manager – no degree was even necessary for employment, according to Labor Department occupation descriptions. Among those three positions, office manager was the top-paying, at $44,300.

Although a degree in psychology might prove helpful in working with people in these types of jobs, the knowledge of psychology gained from such a degree isn't necessary to land these jobs. That would seem to raise questions about the actual value these workers got from their psychology degree. Again, we should point out that we are framing our discussion strictly in terms of the perhaps crass but oh so important *monetary* value of knowledge.

Administrative assistant and customer service representative also are among the 10 jobs most frequently held by graduates with bachelor's degrees in history. In fact, aside from high school teacher and middle school teacher, none of the jobs that made the top 10 seemed to require a good grasp of history. Only three of the jobs had median pay above $50,000: retail store manager ($52,500), non-profit executive director ($64,100) and operations manager ($71,400).

For More Information

The U.S. Bureau of Labor Statistics compiles its Occupational Outlook Handbook every couple of years, providing information on education requirements, earning expectations, job prospects and working conditions for hundreds of occupations. To view the 2010-2011 edition — and its workplace predictions through 2018 — visit www.bls.gov/oco.

Six of the 10 jobs most frequently held by political science majors had median annual earnings above $50,000: paralegal, legal secretary, operations manager, intelligence analyst, employment recruiter and retail store manager. Intelligence analysts had the top median yearly pay at $81,200. Administrative assistant and customer service representative were among the 10 jobs listed for political science majors, as well.

Administrative assistant and customer service representative, which are occupations that employ large numbers of workers, even show up on the list of 10 jobs most frequently held by business majors. But, unlike the other major fields examined, those occupations are the only two on the business major list paying less than $40,000 annually. All the other top jobs for business graduates offer much greater earning potential.

MMV Strategy 3: Find ways to combine your passion with something that has high market value.

Our emphasis on understanding the market value of a degree does not mean that we are advising young people to ignore or bypass less marketable fields, such as history, political science or art, to pursue the better investment bet of a business degree. Given that every student has different passions and aptitudes, that advice would be terrible. It's *not* the greatest idea to choose your career *only* on the basis of expected earnings. But it's also not the greatest idea to choose a career without giving expected earnings any thought. Find a career path that rewards you with what you value – whether that's money, prestige, interaction or leisure – and then figure out a path that makes sense both personally and financially.

If you really love poetry or history or art – and you have aptitude to match that interest – then, by all means, follow your passion. Passion and fulfillment are what make a lifetime of work feel less like a job and more like a joy. But low-paying, unfulfilling jobs outside of their field of interest aren't what most students are envisioning when, with such hope and optimism, they make their college choices. Add an oppressive debt burden to a low-paying, unfulfilling job outside of their field of interest, and the combination can be downright demoralizing.

You have the ability to increase the odds that you won't face such a fate. All you have to do is think creatively and strategically about how you can best apply your skills and interests in the marketplace. If your love is art, graphic design or product design probably offer better odds of financial reward in today's marketplace than trying to break through as a sculptor. The term "struggling artist" didn't develop by accident, after all. Or maybe you're better off finding a mentor to study under one-on-one and taking business courses in college so that you have the skills to manage your career, a gallery or a museum.

Graphic designers, by the way, had a median annual salary of $43,180 in May 2009, according to the BLS. Fine artists – which include painters, sculptors and illustrators – had median earnings of about $44,000, with the top 10 percent making nearly $87,000. But only about 9,000 people were employed as fine artists in the United States in May 2009, compared to 200,870 employed as graphic designers. If you think you could be one of the 9,000 employed artists, go for it. Otherwise, hedge your bets with a more market-oriented approach.

If your passion is writing, then you may want to combine or supplement an English or journalism degree with science or computer science coursework so that you will be positioned to earn good pay as a technical writer while you work on your great American novel. In 2007-2008, more than 55,000 students graduated with a bachelor's degree in English, and more than 76,000 graduated with degrees in communication and journalism. According to the PayScale.com list, technical writer was the highest-paying job among the top 10 occupations for English graduates, at a median salary of $65,700. That would seem to be a much better combining of interest, talent and opportunity than is experienced by the English graduates who wind up working as administrative assistants and office managers for substantially less money.

The reality is that your choice of college major does not lock you into a particular career. The best way for you to improve your career odds and options is to focus on acquiring skills – whatever your major – that are valued in the workplace. That alone should put you ahead of the game.

According to a 2010 study by the National Leadership Council for Liberal Education and America's Promise (LEAP) and the Association of American Colleges and Universities, about 63 percent of employers say college graduates lack the necessary skills to succeed in today's global economy.

Communication and analytical skills were among the essential abilities cited, as was a greater cross-disciplinary awareness. You should work on developing these skills regardless of which major you choose.

We're not suggesting that you choose your career simply on the basis of expected earnings. Remember, money doesn't buy happiness. That said, you shouldn't do the opposite either: pursue any field at any cost without any thought to future earning potential.

Cram Session

- In a knowledge economy, some kinds of knowledge have more market value than other kinds of knowledge.
- Differences in the market value for knowledge are based on two things: the value of the knowledge itself and how much of the knowledge is needed in the economy.
- Completing a college degree tells potential employers not only about your aptitude but also your perseverance.
- The best way for you to improve your career odds and options is to focus on acquiring skills – whatever your major – that are valued in the workplace. That alone should put you ahead of the game.

Key Concepts:
financial aid
Expected Family Contribution
FAFSA (Free Application for Federal Student Aid)

Chapter 6
Strategies for Financing College & Keeping Debt Under Control

So far, we have avoided a difficult subject associated with the college decision – how to finance the investment. This is an extremely complex topic, and the complexity is why so many families get in over their heads. Before we talk about financing the education investment, let's talk about financing large family investments in general.

Probably the two largest investments of resources for many families are a car (or cars) and a house. Putting aside the peculiarities of the mortgage crisis and the 2008 financial collapse, let's look at a few numbers regarding the relationship between what families earn and what most reasonable lenders generally are willing to loan.

Most online debt calculators will return similar numbers. The calculations aren't exact, but they are in the right ballpark. What you should notice about this table

What Banks Will Generally Let You Borrow		
	For a House	For a Car
$30,000 Household Income	$90,000	$20,000
$40,000 Household Income	$120,000	$26,000
$50,000 Household Income	$150,000	$32,000
$60,000 Household Income	$200,000	$38,000

is that, in general, *the more money you have, the more money you can borrow.* People who have lower incomes are more limited in their borrowing capacity than people with higher incomes. Banks and other lenders make this a fairly standard rule because it increases the likelihood that they will get their money back. Lenders who allow applicants to borrow more than they can afford risk losing their money if borrowers end up not being able to make the payments.

Here is how higher education is absolutely unique: In the wacky world of financial aid, the less money you have in hand to pay your out-of-pocket expenses for college, the *more* you are eligible to borrow. (Notice we said "borrow." We aren't talking about scholarships and grants here.) In other words, people with lower incomes are often invited to dig bigger financial holes for themselves.

We know that this seems like a very strange thing to say, and we recognize that there are good intentions behind this practice. Higher education is a path to a better-paying job and presumably a better life. Student loans provide access for families who otherwise might not be able to afford college and the opportunities that a college education brings. That's the positive side of student loans. But the all-too-frequent dark side is that students and families are encouraged and allowed to take on more college debt than is wise, given the payback they are likely to see. Let's return to Sam and his college choices so you can see what we mean.

Recall that Sam had four college options. College A is the lovely – but pricey – private college that he really wants to attend. Let's assume that Sam used some of our advice to bring down the total out-of-pocket price tag for his four-year college degree. Let's say he managed to get credit for 15 hours of dual-enrollment classes and planned to take 18 hours instead of the standard 15 for five semesters. Those two strategies (assuming that College A advisers are cooperative) would cut his time to a bachelor's degree by a full year of school and would reduce his out-of-pocket cost

Definition

Expected Family Contribution – The Expected Family Contribution is based on the information that your family provides in the FAFSA (the Free Application for Federal Student Aid). All families who hope to receive grants, student loans or many kinds of scholarships will have to fill out this form. This will be a yearly ordeal for as long as you are in college. The amount of financial aid that you are eligible for is based on your family's annual household income, the number of people in your family and the amount of assets that you and your family have. Based on these numbers, the government calculates what it thinks your family should be able to pay. This is your Expected Family Contribution. This is a complex calculation. The website www.finaid.org provides an EFC calculator, but it first points out a number of caveats about its methodology and assumptions. As a rough rule of thumb, middle-income families can assume that their Expected Family Contribution for each year will be around 10 percent to 20 percent of the Adjusted Gross Income for the parents, plus 20 percent of total assets that the student may have accumulated. Families with incomes below $60,000 will likely be expected to contribute less than 10 percent, while households with higher incomes pay more. If a family has an adjusted gross household income of $60,000, the parents would be expected to cover about $6,500 per year (or about $26,000 over four years). If the student has $10,000 in a college savings account, he or she would be expected to fork over about $2,000 per year. Families with adjusted gross income of $100,000 and $60,000 in assets would be expected to contribute about $18,000 per year. For these calculations, we used the www.finaid.org EFC calculator and assumed a family of four, with one child in college and with the age of the older parent being 48.

for College A to about $71,000. That's a significant reduction, but he and his family would still need to come up with $71,000.

As Sam's family starts to figure out the financing

for the college investment, the first thing they will need to do is fill out a government form called the FAFSA (Free Application for Federal Student Aid). This is a form that is probably even more complicated than the family income tax form! The FAFSA collects information on family and student assets and income, and that information is used to determine, based on a formula, how much the family can afford to contribute to the education investment. This is called the "Expected Family Contribution." The more money you have, the more your family is expected to contribute. To get grants, student loans and many scholarships, your family will have to fill out the FAFSA form every year you are in college.

The table below shows the four college choice scenarios that we looked at before and three possible household incomes for Sam's family. You can see that the college financing decision doesn't look much like other large family investments and purchases. Remember the car loans and mortgages? With those purchases, the less you make, the less you can borrow. But, as you can see from the table, *the way college loan eligibility is calculated, the **less***

How Much Would Sam Be Allowed to Borrow?				
	College A	College B	College C	College D
TOTAL Education Investment (Reduced by EI Strategies)	$70,560	$72,105	$37,740	$23,076
Assume $70,000 Per Year Parent Household Income Expected FAMILY Contribution (4 years)	$35,600	$35,600	$35,600	$35,600
Student Loan Eligibility Maximum	**$34,960**	**$36,505**	**$2,140**	**$0**
Assume $60,000 Per Year Parent Household Income Expected FAMILY Contribution (4 years)	$26,000	$26,000	$26,000	$26,000
Student Loan Eligibility Maximum	**$44,560**	**$46,105**	**$11,740**	**$0**
Assume $50,000 Per Year Parent Household Income Expected FAMILY Contribution (4 years)	$20,000	$20,000	$20,000	$20,000
Student Loan Eligibility Maximum	**$50,560**	**$52,105**	**$17,740**	**$3,076**

money families make, the ***more*** *they are eligible to borrow using federal education loans.*

Financing Four Years of College

If Sam's parents have an income of around $50,000 per year, the government agencies that come up with the rules say that the family is expected to contribute about $20,000 over the four years. But Sam and his family can use "financial aid," also called "student loans," to *borrow* the remaining $50,560 needed to pay for College A. If Sam's parents have an income of $60,000 per year, they are expected to come up with about $26,000 from their own bank account and are only eligible for student loans in the amount of about $45,000.

Regardless of income, Sam and his family will be on the hook for close to $71,000, whether paid upfront or financed over time, if he chooses College A – and graduates in four years. If Sam and his family are price sensitive and decide to go with College D, *they will be eligible to borrow* ***much less*** *money than if they were to go with the more expensive option.* This is another weird aspect of the whole financial aid process.

The convoluted logic of financial aid is what keeps parents up at night as their prospective students ponder

Strategy Tip

Don't get sucked in! Financial aid advisers at expensive colleges like to show prospective students how much money they are eligible for. It looks really impressive when, at a $35,000-per-year college, you are told you can get up to, say, $18,000 in loans and grants per year. The adviser will then show you that you might only be eligible for $5,000 per year in loans at a Noname Regional State University. For some reason, families often think that the first option is a "better deal" because they get so much more money. NO! The families aren't getting the money, the COLLEGE is! Unless the money is coming in the form of grants or scholarships, you will have to pay it back. It's not free.

their college choices. The rules of thumb for financial aid seem to be the opposite of financing rules for cars and houses. Generally, for those big-ticket purchases, banks try to keep people from borrowing more than they can afford. No one, not the college, not the government, not the financial aid adviser, ever seems to say that the debt level needed for a particular college choice is more than a student and his or her family can afford. Since no one else seems to be saying it, we will. We're not saying a college degree is out of reach. But the price tag for a bachelor's degree at some colleges is, without a doubt, out of reach for many middle-income families. That may seem harsh, but it's true.

What Does This Mean for You?

The bottom line is, if you are an average family with an average income and average bills, you have two choices:

1) You and your parents can take on a substantial amount of debt or

2) You can scale down your college search to focus on places that fit your family's financial circumstances.

Financing Strategy 1: Don't take on more debt for a college education than you and your family can afford!

Most students and their families fund the college investment with money that could be used for other purposes. Very few students have a large pile of cash in the bank to be used exclusively for college. Many families use personal savings, loans against home equity, loans against retirement and credit cards to put together the payments necessary for their daughters or sons to go to college. In addition, students access credit cards and student loan programs with the expectation that they will have the money in the future to repay whatever amount they borrow.

It is *very* likely that you and your family are going to have to borrow some money before you finish your college degree. Our advice to help keep debt in perspective is to think in terms of a new car. How much would you, or your mom and dad, be willing to spend on a new car? If you think that spending $100,000 is too much for a college student's car, maybe it's too much for a college education investment.

Financing for the college investment is hard to figure out. And it is incredibly easy to run up extremely large bills that will eventually have to be paid. At the same time, it is *really* unlikely in the current economic climate that a typical American family has easy access to the amount of ready cash that the government calculation of Expected Family Contribution says you should have. Maybe your family has the money in hand. If so, you are one of the lucky ones. Given that many families are living paycheck to paycheck, with their mortgages underwater and their retirement accounts underfunded, it is a real challenge to generate the extra money every semester to cover college expenses for four or five years.

What Does This Mean for You?

Here is the big picture perspective: Parents who may need to get serious about saving for retirement or grandparents who need to conserve resources for health care shouldn't be using their purchasing power for a college degree UNLESS they AREN'T going to need the money themselves.

Evaluating the Options

Let's say Sam's family, for reasons of illness, job interruptions, bad investments, poor planning or any number of other challenges, doesn't have a huge pot of money set aside for his schooling. This isn't uncommon. Suppose between savings, extra income from picking up overtime hours and a few sacrifices, Sam's family has $8,000 in some form of cash for his education (this is about $2,000 per year). Remember, we are looking at the big picture, so try to think in terms of at least four years.

If you look at our table, you can see that if Sam's parents make $50,000 per year, their expected contribution is going to be about $20,000. So, if they have $8,000 on hand, that means they are still going to have to come up with another $12,000 from somewhere. This is *even before* Sam starts taking out government-backed student loans to cover the remaining almost $51,000 that it will take to keep Sam in College A for the four years. Between Sam and his parents, that is a total of $63,000 ($12,000 + $51,000) in borrowed money. That could buy a *really* nice car! Putting that into perspective in another way, to finance the college education, Sam and his family will need to borrow more than the family *earns in a year!*

Let's think about the best-case scenario: Even if Sam's parents already have the $20,000 that the government calculation says they will need to kick in for the four years of Sam's college education, there will *still* be another $51,000 in borrowing necessary. Remember, using our numbers, this is *after* Sam has gotten a scholarship for College A and *after* working really hard to bring down the total price of the college degree by getting dual-enrollment credit and by planning to take 18 hours for five semesters while he's there. The irony is that if Sam chooses the least costly option, College D, based on the rules for financial aid, he's probably not going to be eligible for much government-backed loan money. Because of their $50,000 income, the family will still be expected to contribute $20,000 to the cost of college over the four years. Assuming that Sam's parents have $8,000 to spend on college, they will still have to come up with another $12,000 over the four years to invest in his bachelor's degree. And Sam may need to borrow about $3,100 to cover the remaining cost. Both Sam and his parents will be burdened with some debt, but, at this level, the sacrifice doesn't seem like too high a price to pay for a degree that may improve Sam's earning potential and help insulate him from unemployment.

If your family is like most, choosing a school like College A or B will mean that you can expect to leave school saddled with a large amount of debt. Even the less expensive Colleges C and D will require significant financial commitments from your family. Assuming that your circumstances remain the same – meaning that your parents don't win the lottery or you don't have a wealthy uncle die, leaving you untold riches – there is a very strong chance that you will leave school owing money. You may owe the federal government, a private bank or a credit card company, but you'll likely owe someone.

Financing Strategy 2: Get a clear idea of what the total (not yearly) amount of debt will be for the education investment *before* you make a commitment to accept admission to a college or university.

When you and your parents start to think about financing the investment in a college education, it is really important to project the *total* amount of money that you will need to borrow. Let's look at an example from the business world. In business, we know that the reason most small businesses fail is because they are undercapitalized, meaning that the owner didn't really have enough money to get the business up and running. In other words, running the business cost more than the owner thought it would. The same type of thing happens with the college investment.

It doesn't sound so bad when a financial aid adviser puts you down for a loan of $7,000 in your freshman year. But if you take five years to graduate and you keep that level of financial need, the bill you get as you walk off stage with your bachelor's degree will be $35,000! At some point, your parents may realize that they are financially in over their heads, and you, the student, may end up having

Definitions

Grants – Grants, unlike loans, do not have to be repaid. Visit the link below to learn more about grant programs available for eligible students pursuing a postsecondary education.

http://studentaid.ed.gov/PORTALSWebApp/students/english/grants.jsp

Campus-Based Aid – The Federal Supplemental Educational Opportunity Grant (FSEOG), Federal Work-Study (FWS), and Federal Perkins Loan are called campus-based programs because they're administered directly by the financial aid office at each participating school. Not all schools participate in all three programs. Check with your school's financial aid office to find out which programs they participate in. To learn more, visit:

http://studentaid.ed.gov/PORTALSWebApp/students/english/
campusaid.jsp

Direct Stafford Loans – Direct Stafford Loans, from the William D. Ford Federal Direct Loan Program, are low-interest loans for eligible students to help cover the cost of higher education at a four-year college or university, community college, or trade, career, or technical school. Eligible students borrow directly from the U.S. Department of Education at participating schools.

http://studentaid.ed.gov/PORTALSWebApp/students/english/student-loans.jsp

Direct PLUS Loans for Parents – Parents of dependent students may apply for a Direct PLUS Loan to help pay their child's education expenses as long as certain eligibility requirements are met. Visit:

http://studentaid.ed.gov/PORTALSWebApp/students/english/parent-loans.jsp

Private Student Loans –Private student loans (also known as alternative student loans or personal student loans) can help you pay for college, generally at better interest rates than other lines of credit. In 2010, President Obama signed into law a plan to have the federal government take the place of private banks in providing student loans.

http://www.salliemae.com/NR/exeres/5ECFBBCC-72BA-4201-95D7-0CE8B498C0B0.htm

Definitions from: Federal Student Aid – www.studentaid.ed.gov

to leave school because it just isn't affordable. As with the small business owner who underestimated the true necessary cost, your college venture would turn out to be undercapitalized.

How Much Do Families Tend to Owe?

As we've noted before, about two-thirds of students who graduate from a four-year college leave with loan debt, according to the Project on Student Debt. In 2008, undergraduate students who borrowed left school owing, on average, $23,200. That's quite a lot of money for a 22-year-old just starting out in the job market to owe, but it does fall within our rule of thumb that college debt not exceed what would be a reasonable price for you to pay for a new car. However, the $23,200 average in student loans *underrepresents* the total amount of debt a student and his or her family might have. The $23,000 borrowing average includes only federal and non-federal loans that are held by a *student* and that are accounted for in government reports. As far as the student's debt level is concerned, that number doesn't include any credit card debt used to pay for tuition, room and board, books or supplies. Credit cards are the biggest debt trap of all for young people, who are often charged interest rates above 20 percent.

In reality, the $23,200 average debt load is often just the tip of the iceberg. That's because this "average" debt load significantly masks the total debt *families* are taking on for higher education because *it doesn't include parent loans.* A 2010 College Board report called "Who Borrows Most? Bachelor's Degree Recipients With High Levels of Student Debt" found that, among students who took on high levels of debt, *the average federal Parents Loan for Undergraduate Students (PLUS) was $30,900!*

It isn't just lower income families who are piling on the debt. Nearly 50 percent of parent households earning

$60,000 or more took on PLUS debt. Among households with incomes of $100,000 or more who took on debt, *47 percent borrowed an average $41,500 through the federal PLUS program.* The report noted that these loans were in addition to the $30,500 or more taken on by student borrowers who graduate with higher than average levels of debt. The final piece of the hidden debt iceberg is that even these large amounts *don't include* any home equity loans or other sources of credit (like credit cards) that parents may have tapped to pay for the college investment.

It's safe to assume that the total amount of debt families are incurring for college is *significantly* underreported. As we've said before, the college decision isn't just about you, the student; it's a family decision because it is a significant allocation of family resources. Investing so much of your family's financial resources in one undergraduate bachelor's degree may not be the best decision for your family as a whole.

Yes, this flies in the face of the tradition that parents and grandparents sacrifice for the younger generation. But times are different now. People are living longer, health care is increasingly expensive, and returns from stock market investments (if you are lucky enough to have them) are erratic and unreliable. It isn't an easy decision, but the uncertain economy suggests that parents and grandparents must be more conservative in their financial decisions. They can't rely on the notion – in reality, they probably never really could – that their home or stock investments will appreciate enough to make up for any debts. Keeping the price tag for college in line with the resources of the family will reduce financial stresses for everyone in the long run.

Although you need to think in terms of the total amount of borrowing that will be necessary, you also need to think about the impact of all this borrowing on your finances and opportunities down the road – *after* college.

Financing Strategy 3: Before you commit to a college, know how much your monthly payment on your total loan obligation is likely to be after graduation.

In business, there is a term called "cash flow." For a business to be successful, it has to have a positive cash flow. This means that regardless of how much debt the business has, as long as the company can generate enough revenue to cover its operating costs plus pay off debt, it can usually stay in business. Not getting enough cash in the door is another common reason that companies fail.

For you, at 18 or 19 and thinking about college life and not the work world, the idea of cash flow may not seem relevant. But remember, we're trying to get you to think about the big picture. When it comes to planning for college, you can't just think about your life as it is now. You also have to think five years down the road. When you are finished with college, will you have the monthly cash flow that you will need to pay back your college loans?

Figuring out your student loan payment in the future is another example of how financial aid looks *nothing* like a car payment or a mortgage payment. In an attempt to make you feel comfortable borrowing money to invest in a college education, the federal government has created a laundry list of repayment options. Although this has helped a lot of people manage the monthly payment, it doesn't change the fact that *the longer you take to pay a loan off, the more it is going to cost you.* This is because interest on the loans accumulates and increases over time.

How Much Will You Have
to Pay Every Month?

Let's go back to Sam and his financial choices. Remember that if he went to College A and his parents gave him $20,000, even if he employed strategies to bring down the costs, he would still have to borrow about $51,000 to get his bachelor's degree. Let's go back to our discussion in Chapter 5 and assume the best-case scenario: Sam graduates in a timely fashion and gets a job making $47,000. At 6.8 percent interest on $51,000 in student loans over a 10-year timeframe, Sam could expect a monthly payment of about $587. The total amount that Sam would pay over the 10 years of his loan would be $70,429. That means interest alone would total $19,429. Although $587 is not an outrageous sum per month, the payment would take a significant bite out of Sam's paycheck. After taxes, Sam would be taking home about $2,800 per month. About 18 percent of that each month would have to go toward repaying his student loans.

There is some good news related to student loan repayment, though. As of 2009, someone like Sam can qualify for an "Income-Based Repayment Plan." (You can learn more about this at www.ibrinfo.org). This is a federal government program that tries to help student borrowers keep their loan payments manageable. Generally, if your annual income after graduation is less than about $60,000, you can qualify for this program. Based on the IBR calculator, Sam's $51,000 loan would require a $380 payment per month. This would be about 13 percent of his take-home pay.

Before you breathe a sigh of relief on behalf of Sam, you need to know that the trade-off is that it would take Sam 21 years to repay his college loan debt. Extending the payoff timeframe from 10 to 21 years would increase the total cost of the loan to $95,922, with $44,922 of that amount in interest. Sam would be in his 40s by the time he paid off the debt he incurred as an 18- to 22-year-old. By then, he might even have kids of his own who were starting to look at ways to pay for college!

If Sam got all of his loans through the government, this is the kind of monthly obligation he could expect. Government loan repayment would be the cheapest way to go from a cash flow point of view. If he had a mix of government, private and credit card debt, which would not be unlikely, his repayment would be affected by the varying interest rates, and his month-to-month obligation most certainly would be higher.

We know that this all may seem *very* confusing, but our basic point is simple: Take the time to know the potential impact of your college debt obligation on your future cash flow. The amount you have to pay back every month may have implications for the kind of job you decide to take, the kind of car you drive, the kind of house you buy, when you get married and even whether you decide to continue your education.

More than 40 percent of students who don't go on to graduate school blame debt, according to the Project on Student Debt. More than half of all former students who borrowed money say they would borrow less if they could do it all over again. More than likely, you and your family are going to have to borrow money to complete your college education. We just want you to make sure you know what you are getting into before you sign on the dotted line.

Cram Session

- The way college loan eligibility is calculated, the LESS money families make, the MORE they are eligible to borrow using federal education loans.
- As of 2009, the federal government launched the "Income-Based Repayment Plan," which tries to help student borrowers keep their loan payments manageable.
- More than 40 percent of students who don't go on to graduate school blame debt.
- More than half of all former students who borrowed money say they would borrow less if they could do it all over again.

Key Concepts:
graduation rate
time management
syllabus
Family Educational Rights and Privacy Act (FERPA)

Chapter 7
Get to Graduation: Strategies for Earning the Degree

If you aren't already a bit shell-shocked from reading about the size of the college investment, we have another piece of reality for you to think about. As difficult as it is to finance your college investment, it is even harder to see real financial benefit from it! Why? On average, the six-year graduation rate for colleges and universities is a little better than 50 percent. What this means is that for every two college freshmen who start at a particular college this year, only one will actually have graduated from that same school six years from now.

A college degree differs from other purchases in that you don't actually get to have the market value of it until the very end. If you go to college for three years and only have a year left, you don't get credit in the job market for much more than a high school diploma. *Finishing is absolutely fundamental to making this investment pay off.*

Although it is in the best interest of everyone – the college, you, your family and society at large – that you complete your degree, the fact is, unlike high school, colleges are not set up to make sure that you graduate. As a matter of fact, until recently, colleges didn't care all that much about their graduation rates. Instead, the mentality was more of a "survival of the fittest" approach. Once a student was in, it was largely up to her or him to figure out how to get through to the end.

As we've already said, more people than ever are going to college, but the reality is that colleges were never set up to attract or educate everyone. Traditionally, colleges were created for the elite – for the people who had the financial resources (a lot of money) or the people who had a lot of academic talent or the really fortunate ones who had both. Because, until relatively recently, most people didn't need college degrees, these institutions tended to attract only those people who really wanted to go. Even when the GI Bill enabled soldiers to go to colleges and universities after World War II, only a relatively small percentage took advantage of the opportunity to get a degree. According to the U.S. Census, in 1952 (seven years after the end of World War II), only about 6 percent of people over the age of 25 had a college degree.

Although the economy has changed dramatically over the years, creating more demand than ever for a college degree, not much has changed inside many colleges and universities. Most still are designed for students with lots of academic talent, lots of money or both.

Colleges are starting to pay more attention to graduation rates, but most haven't found any magic bullet (or effective strategy) to transform the average 21st century high school senior into a college grad. This isn't meant (at least not entirely) as an indictment of the current system. Instead, we want to make sure you understand that the challenge doesn't end when you finally get that acceptance letter in your hand. That's when the real obstacle course toward your goal begins. For far too many students, getting into college turns out to be the easy part. Graduating is tough.

Getting to Graduation (GTG)

The first step toward increasing the probability that you make it to graduation is to accept the fact that your college investment is mostly riding on your young shoulders. There are plenty of books that can give you ideas about study skills and time management. What we want you to think about here is the big picture, and that goes beyond tactics such as making sure you know where the library is. So beyond the obvious advice about avoiding sex, drugs, booze and rock and roll (if it makes you more inclined to the other three), what are some things you can do to avoid the temptations and pitfalls that seem to be built into the college system?

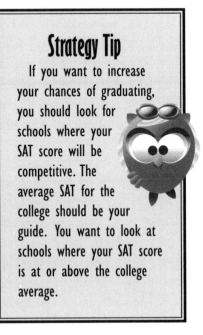

Strategy Tip

If you want to increase your chances of graduating, you should look for schools where your SAT score will be competitive. The average SAT for the college should be your guide. You want to look at schools where your SAT score is at or above the college average.

GTG Strategy 1: Minimize major changes.

We've already talked about the importance of having a career in mind when you start your college program. Having at least some sense of what you might like to do and what you might earn for doing it helps you narrow your college search to schools that offer reasonable payback potential. But taking the time to think about what you really might like to do also will help you avoid costly and time-consuming major changes.

In many respects, undergraduate academic majors at colleges and universities, especially those in the humanities, haven't changed much in the last 100 years. Majors are predefined sets of requirements that you have to meet to receive a degree in a particular subject. Students who move from major to major inside a university are often sur-

Strategy Tip

If you find yourself halfway through your junior year and you decide that you don't love, or even much like, the field that you have chosen, think long and hard before you switch majors. That's just going to reset your college clock and potentially make it less likely that you will finish. As long as your major isn't putting you at risk of flunking out or dropping out, stay the course.

Use your electives to allow you to explore areas that may interest you more or that will make you more marketable. Look for opportunities to develop marketable skills in areas in which you may want to work. For example, if you're a psychology major and, three years in, you suddenly have an epiphany that graphic arts is your calling, stick with the psychology. You've already invested your time. Besides, psychology may come in handy as you start to navigate challenging personalities in the workplace. Instead, supplement your classroom experience with internship opportunities, part-time work or volunteer activities. Offer to put together the church newsletter or to design a flier for your friend's band gig. Take a few extra elective classes in graphic arts without going for the degree.

Unless you can be sure that you are willing to stick around an extra semester, year or even two, don't switch out of your program. Remember, the primary objective is the degree. Any degree is better than none.

prised at *how few* courses count from one major to another. And just so you know, it is *very* common for young people to change their minds about their college majors – many more than once.

But each time you change your mind about whether you want to be a chemical engineer or a pharmacist, an interior designer or a journalist, you run the risk that the change will cost you in time and in money. Although you likely have flexibility in the first year to rethink and make adjustments, the deeper you go in your major program, the harder it will be to switch. The more time you take, the more money you spend. Sometimes students run out of money before they run out of requirements. For example, scholarships and grants often are awarded for a maximum of four years. If you go beyond that timeframe, for whatever reason, you might lose that source of funding.

You will have to weigh the pros and cons of this for yourself, but before you pull the plug on two or more years of investment in a particular field, see if you can retool your study path with an internship or by taking extra classes outside your major.

GTG Strategy 2: Better to slow down than to stop.

Another potential temptation that keeps students from the graduation ceremony is the "stop-out." Stop-out refers to when students decide to take a year or two off after they've already started college. It's called stop-out because students don't really intend to "drop out"; they intend to return. There are lots of reasons why students stop-out: money, grades, family problems, pregnancy, general unhappiness with college life or lack of direction, among others. But many stop-out students learn that it is much harder to restart their college journey once they have stopped. Despite the best intentions, these stop-outs often turn into college drop-outs.

If you find yourself facing a difficult hurdle in life and are contemplating temporarily stopping your college journey, try slowing down instead. Yes, we know this seems to run counter to our advice about trying to minimize your time to a degree in order to maximize the return on your college investment. But life sometimes gets in the way of even the best-laid plans. So, one way to respond to such challenges is to take it slow.

Serious climbers will tell you that slow and steady is

how you get to the top of any mountain. That advice holds true whether the mountain is a physical or mental challenge. If you find yourself facing a financial, academic or personal hurdle that seems too tough to overcome and you're thinking of breaking off your college climb, first give yourself time to acclimate and adjust to this new uneven footing. You may find it's not as bad as you thought.

If you're able to stay in your college town, look into your school's part-time programs. If you have to leave the area and go back to your hometown or to some other location, look for a college close by where you can keep working on your degree. If you eventually go back to your original university, many of these credits (we would hope all) should transfer. (Improve the odds that these credits will count by talking to an adviser about your determination to persevere.) If there isn't a college or university close by, explore online options from your closest public university.

Even if it's only three credits a semester, *keep going!*

GTG Strategy 3: Guard your GPA.

Many students experience a rude awakening when they find out how interested potential employers are in their GPA. At this point, you may not be thinking about how your grades in freshman classes may affect your employability. But graduating with a low grade-point average will make it even harder for you to land a job that will make the return on your college investment worth it.

Students often find that it is easy to blow their GPA and much harder to bring it back. (Debt tends to be a lot like that, as well. People find it much easier to get into than out of debt.) To be in the hunt for a good job after graduation, you need to try to keep at least a 3.0 GPA. That is a "B" average – a college "B" average. Maintaining a "B" average in college may seem much harder than keeping a "B" in your high school classes. That's partly because college classes tend to be more challenging and partly because you tend to take fewer classes in college than in high school. That gives you fewer options for offsetting a bad grade in biology with a great grade in band.

Even if you think it's too soon to worry about your future job prospects, you still have to pay attention to your GPA. Many universities have "student progress" requirements that prevent graduation if you have less than a 2.0 GPA (a "C" average). If your GPA remains below 2.0 for too long, you might find yourself on academic probation or, even worse, suspended.

Although students never intend to get into trouble with their GPA, many fail to realize its importance until it is almost too late to recover. Every year there are students who find out that the junior internship in New York City that they really want or the study-abroad program in Spain that they have been dreaming about is out of reach because their GPA is still hung over from too much partying their freshman year. And imagine the surprise of some 32-year-old applying to grad school who gets wait-listed because her GPA from 10 years earlier isn't high enough for admission to her master's program of choice.

So, even now, at the beginning of your college journey, you have to keep the big picture in mind. What you want as a senior (lots of job offers) is affected by what you do from the moment you set foot on campus. And don't expect Mom or Dad to come to your rescue if you find your grades in trouble.

Parents, especially those out in the suburbs, have grown accustomed to online tools that allow them to check grades and take action at the first hint that their children's grades are suffering. But in college, they won't have such access to monitor your homework and test taking. That's because, at age 18, you're considered an adult and entitled to your privacy.

Because of a law called FERPA – the Family Educational Rights and Privacy Act – colleges and universities are prohibited from telling your parents *anything* about your grades, even though your parents may be paying your bills and have a vested interest in your progress. (Of course, colleges and universities *are* allowed to communicate with your parents about your tuition bill.) So if catastrophe strikes and you come home with a 1.0 GPA for your first semester, Mom and Dad aren't going to be able to call your professors and plead your case. *You are on your own!*

So, now that you know the short-term and long-term consequences, how do you guard your GPA? You start before you even step foot inside the classroom. You should be thinking about your GPA as you weigh your college choices. You do not want to choose a school where you will be continually struggling to maintain a good grade-point average. For example, if a party atmosphere is likely to distract you, you should consider a less raucous environment. Don't make your choice based on Princeton Review's list of Top 20 Party Schools. If you are an average student, then don't shoot for the Ivy League. It's better to be a successful fish in a smaller pond.

After you have made the choice about where to go, guarding your GPA should then figure into what you choose to study. If you freeze at the sight of math, look for majors where you minimize the number of required "numbers" classes. If you're a night owl, don't schedule an 8 a.m. class that you're likely to sleep through. On the other hand, if you typically get groggy in the afternoon despite a stout pot of coffee, try to schedule your classes at a time when you are more alert. If you have a semester in which you need to take one or two classes that you know are going to be really difficult for you, such as organic chemistry or statistics, try to balance those hard classes out with a gut course or two. A "gut" class is any course that, because of subject matter or the professor's requirements, is expected to be an "easy

A." Gut classes vary from school to school. You may need to talk to some upperclassmen to find out what they are. But be forewarned: The class that is thought to be an "easy A" frequently turns out to be more work than expected.

If you get into a class and start to struggle, find a tutor. Join a study group or start one. Haunt the professor. Ask for help. Don't wait until you've already failed the first test. Be proactive. It's your GPA. Protect it!

GTG Strategy 4: Manage your semester – use your syllabus!

Although the whole college experience will be new to you, those of us who see students year after year see the same mistakes over and over. Freshmen are especially vulnerable because they are making a transition from high school study habits to college study habits.

The first important thing to pay attention to in your college course is the syllabus that each professor provides. You may not know this, but the syllabus is a contract between you and the professor. There is more emphasis on the syllabus in undergraduate education than ever before. Accreditation and accountability are really pushing professors to make sure that what is on the syllabus is what happens in class. The syllabus is the key to success in any class, and managing multiple syllabuses is the first critical skill you have to learn.

The syllabus for each class is your scheduling and time-management tool. Exam dates, due dates for papers, rules for attendance and a host of other things are spelled out in the syllabus. You know in the very first week of class exactly what you will have to do for the next 16 weeks (or 10 weeks if you're on quarters). Take advantage of this! Put all of your syllabuses together in the very first week and get a sense of when you are going to have "crunch time" and when you will have some breathing room.

Students complain every year that faculty always give exams around the same time. Duh! Midterm and the two weeks before finals are guaranteed to be busy. If you know this ahead of time, you can make sure to build in extra study time for those busier periods.

In addition to anticipating busy weeks, lining up your syllabuses at the beginning of the semester will give you a sense of how tough your classes are going to be. This is where your syllabus can help you manage your GPA. After looking at all your syllabuses together – and getting a sense of the demands and expectations of each professor and how easy or hard it will be for you to meet all of them – you can assess whether this is the right mix of courses for you. Perhaps you would be better off trading one demanding class this semester for one that will require less time. Then, if need be, pick up the class you dropped during a later semester, when you have a lighter course load or you are better adjusted to the demands of college. Usually, you can only swap one class for another during the first week of the term. After the drop/add period is over, you can only drop a course; you can't exchange.

The advice here is to avoid the all-too-common pitfall of looking at each course syllabus separately. Instead, take a big picture view and see them as a *set* of tasks you have to complete over the academic term. This will help improve the odds that you make good choices about how to spend your time. And maybe, just maybe, you'll even plan ahead for that week when you have three papers due and a test scheduled, instead of panicking last minute and trying to wedge weeks' worth of work into an all-nighter.

We know this sounds incredibly basic, but learning to manage your syllabuses is going to help you manage in real life.

GTG Strategy 5: Make your college career your full-time job.

One mistake that prevents students from getting to graduation is thinking that their college work is a part-time, rather than a full-time, job. College classes are scheduled differently than high school, and sometimes it seems to students that they have enough free time to take on 20, 30 or even 40 hours of work outside of their college courses. *Big mistake!*

We know that the temptation to work is a big one, especially because college costs so much. But college is a full-time commitment. If you are really talented academically, you may be able to keep that 3.0 GPA while also working 30 hours a week; participating in a sport, club or other activity; and having an active social life. But most students *can't* manage all of this.

Remember, if you want to get the best return on your college investment, your focus should be on graduating in the shortest amount of time with a good GPA. Research shows that students routinely put in a lot of hours in jobs outside the college campus. Research also shows that making such an investment of time ultimately costs students in terms of their college investment.

What Does This Mean for You?

Students who work pay a price.

- Forty-six percent of all full-time students who work spend 25 or more hours per week on the job.
- Forty-two percent of these students reported that working hurt their grades.
- Fifty-three percent of all full-time students who work 25 or more hours per week reported that employment limited their class schedule, and 38 percent said that work limited their class choice.
- One in five full-time students who work spends 35 or more hours per week on the job.

Strategy Tips

If you are a student who struggles, here are some steps you can take to improve your odds of making it to the finish line — graduation.

• Take your time. If you have trouble with academics, but you have the financing, take a lighter class load. Focusing on only four classes a semester might help you manage your work more effectively. Carefully managing your financial fund may make it possible for you to plan on a five- or six-year stretch. Remember, the ultimate goal is finishing.

• Keep it small. Whether private or public, go for the small campus (not just small class size).

• Ask for help. Many regional public universities offer remedial services in reading, math and study strategies. You just have to look for them.

• Focus on personal development. Work for free on things that might help you figure out the first direction you want to take. Professors at smaller regional schools tend to be more accessible to undergraduate students because they almost never have teaching assistants or research assistants. Find the Student Services Center at the university and volunteer.

Think about the big picture: If you land a job paying $8 per hour, the difference between working 30 hours a week and 20 hours a week will be about $1,800 after taxes over the course of an academic year. If those 10 extra hours each week mean that you end up going an extra semester or an extra year because your work life ate into your college schedule, then those 10 hours actually cost you money. An extra semester costs a lot more than $1,800. If working those 10 extra hours each week results in your GPA plummeting from a 3.0 to a 2.4, it could cost you even more in the job market after you graduate.

Colleges and universities talk quite a bit these days about developing critical thinkers. Well, critical thinkers understand that sometimes a short-term sacrifice is necessary for long-term gain. Consider this a chance to hone your critical-thinking skills. Before you decide to stretch yourself thin by taking on more work hours than you can manage, try stretching your dollars. Give up your daily Starbucks habit, find a cheaper cell phone plan, slice one pizza run from your weekly routine. If you live off campus, get a roommate or even two, learn to cook and eat at home, or bike to class to save on parking and gas. Cut back and make your college career your full-time commitment. This will improve the odds that you make it to graduation – and make it in a reasonable amount of time.

Make a Plan

The upshot of this advice is that you need to make a plan for finishing – and that planning needs to take place at the very beginning of your college career. Far too many students view their college career as a succession of semesters (or quarters). At the end of one, they start all over again with a new one. That is very short-sighted. Plenty of students find themselves in school for an extra semester, an extra year or even longer because they failed to understand or anticipate something as basic as a school's sequencing of classes. Many higher level classes have prerequisites that must be met before you can take them. Some classes are offered only once a year. If you need the class but don't take it at the time it's offered, then you will be out of luck until it comes around again. No amount of whining about unfairness or pleading about your incredible suffering over a simple mistake will change the course sequencing. Even worse, you will be shut out of any courses and progress that build on that particular class. A little planning ahead can help you avoid such misery.

Too many students treat college as the destination, not as simply part of the journey. And how could they not? So much of what they hear from the time they hit high school

Strategy Tip

Don't assume that your entire college career is going to be like your freshman year. Colleges and universities have been doing backflips to work on making the freshman year fun and engaging. Also, if you have had a pretty strong high school academic experience, some of those freshman classes will seem like easy refresher courses of what you have already studied. Don't let that lull you into a false idea of what college is like. All that investment in the freshman year is about helping convince you to come back for your sophomore year. And guess what? By then, colleges don't think you need any more hand-holding. Those special "freshman" advisers hand you off to the curmudgeonly professor who really doesn't feel any responsibility for your college career. Those "easy" general education classes with the friendly and laid-back profs turn into classes in your major that can be full of high demands, unfamiliar jargon and challenging projects. Expectations that you can graph the elasticity of supply and demand or solve the physics of whether you weigh more going up in an elevator than you do coming down start to crowd out your social life. Party time gives way to "networking" with future employers at career fairs and required attendance at extracurricular talks on worthy topics in your field of study. We hope you think these things sound exciting because this is what you can expect to be doing for the three to five "post-freshman" years it will take to finish your degree.

is what they have to do to get to the promised land of college. But think of college as a long car ride to your new life as an adult. Few people would set off on a solo trip across unfamiliar terrain without first at least mapping out how they plan to get to their destination. They probably won't plot every detail, every stop. But they'll have a general sense of the routes they need to take miles and miles down the road. They'll anticipate the entire journey, not just each individual leg.

Aside from helping you take the right routes to get you where you want to go, planning also helps you anticipate obstacles. Throughout your educational journey thus far, you have probably had people – parents, teachers, guidance counselors – giving you directions and monitoring your progress. But your journey through college – for better or for worse – is largely a solo one. Sure, there are professors who are willing to give advice on direction, there are services to help you find your way, but probably for the first time ever, you alone are in the driver's seat. No one is going to chase you around to make sure you are getting to class, that you are getting enough sleep, that you have not maxed out your credit card. No one is going to "give" you a job at the end. Graduation itself isn't even a given.

The college phase of your journey is thrilling, exciting and transforming. But like any trip into unfamiliar territory, it can be confusing, bumpy and winding. Every year, students get lost along the way. Every year, a lot of really smart, motivated people are missing from that graduation line. They lacked a plan for getting where they wanted to go and getting back on track when they ran into life's inevitable detours. Making it to your destination is up to you. You're in the driver's seat. Get your map. Fasten your seatbelt. And get going.

Cram Session

- Getting to graduation requires planning and commitment.
- Too many students treat college as the destination, not as simply part of the journey.
- The first important thing to pay attention to in your college course is the syllabus that each professor provides. The syllabus for each class is your scheduling and time-management tool.
- If you get into a class and start to struggle, find a tutor. Join a study group or start one. Haunt the professor. Ask for help. Don't wait until you've already failed the first

test. Be proactive. It's YOUR GPA. Protect it!

- Students often find that the temptation to work is a big one, especially because college costs so much. But many find themselves in trouble when their work life gets in the way of what should be their full-time focus – their college education.
- About half of college students change their majors at least once before they graduate.

Part TWO:
Comparison Shopping

Key Concepts:
selectivity
retention rate
six-year graduation rate
success rate

Chapter 8
Understanding Universities: How to Size Up Your Options

You're smart to want to find a college that fits you. Finding an educational environment where you feel comfortable and that suits your needs is important to the learning process. But so much of what is written today in terms of college choice advises you to think about "fit" primarily in intangible, emotional terms. Did you feel welcome on campus? Could you picture yourself there? Did the new dormitories you were shown seem cozy but cool? Did your tour of state-of-the-art facilities leave you impressed?

Make no mistake – colleges spend big money these days trying to ensure that you have a "feel-good" experience when you take your campus tour. The recruitment and admissions process has become a multibillion-dollar industry. That's right, multi*billion*. Schools, especially big public institutions that can't compare to the coziness of small private ones, hire consultants to teach admissions officials and student tour guides exactly what to highlight, right down to the most advantageous spot on campus to stop and answer any questions you may have. Recruiting students, particularly the best and the brightest, is competitive business, and colleges have to do what they need to do. But you should assume a certain amount of staging has gone into every brochure, every visit and every "frank" discussion with a "real" student.

In some ways, the pressure and emphasis on making the "right" college choice is similar to all the frenzy and excess that surrounds planning a wedding nowadays. The fantasy of creating the "perfect" wedding has little bearing on the reality of marriage. Similarly, the fantasy of picking one "best" or "right" college has little connection to the reality of day-to-day life on campus. The intense social pressure to achieve perfection in both endeavors drives many families to spend money in ways they never would for less emotionally charged financial decisions. And think about this: Even if the wedding day or the college choice seemed to have been perfect at the time, the odds of the marriage ending in divorce or the degree going unearned are, on average, nearly 50 percent. Perhaps that means, in both instances, the focus may be too much on the fantasy and not enough on the reality.

Understanding Differences

You already know that colleges differ financially. On paper, there are huge differences in price. You also know that some colleges are considered more academically elite and demanding than others. For some schools, that reputation may be well-earned; for others, it may simply be an "aura" of prestige.

But you have also learned – at least you have if you read Chapter 2 – that, regardless of what advertising materials say, undergraduate programs tend to be very similar. The campus setting, surrounding environment and extracurricular experiences may differ drastically, but the actual undergraduate program, meaning the courses and curriculum, at most campuses are remarkably similar. Because most schools are accredited by the same associations, you can assume that you will receive a comparable education in terms of faculty quality, course content and degree requirements regardless of where you choose to pursue your bachelor's degree. Sure, there will be individual academic strengths, but, at the undergraduate level, these differences are not as critical to the overall learning package as they are at the graduate level.

What you also may not know or fully appreciate is that humans – even brand-name-obsessed college students – are incredibly adaptable beings. A song from 1970s folk rocker Stephen Stills sums up the phenomenon quite nicely: "If you can't be with the one you love, honey, love the one you're with." In other words, even if you end up going to a school that is not your first, second or even fifth choice, you're likely to leave that fall-back choice happy with the experience you had.

The Higher Education Research Institute surveys students about their college satisfaction levels. In HERI's 2008-2009 survey of graduating seniors, more than 95 percent of the 24,000 students who responded said they were satisfied with the general education or core curriculum of their university. This suggests that the vast majority of students leave school relatively happy with their college experience. Even students who thought they were not going to like their school when they first arrived on campus tend to leave relatively content.

So, given the broad similarity in academic programming and this remarkable human ability to adapt, what factors should a discerning student (like you) consider when weighing college options? After 12 years of primary and secondary school, you know all about the 3 R's. When it comes to assessing your higher education options, think about 4 S's:

- **Sticker price**
- **Size**
- **Selectivity**
- **Success rate**

Of all the possible information out there, these four criteria give you the data to narrow your field of choices to those colleges that best match your circumstances and needs. After using these four pieces of information to come up with a short list, you can then turn to more subjective feelings of fit to determine colleges that offer you the best opportunity for success. These four critical criteria should be the starting point for whittling your list of best educational options whether you are considering a private institution, a public university, a community college or a trade school.

Let's start with the most obvious factor that can help narrow your options: sticker price.

Sticker Price

We've already spent an entire chapter of this book on sticker price. But in case you don't believe us when we say that well-educated, middle-income parents frequently make misguided financial moves when it comes to their children's college choices, here is a true story to make the point for us. Consider the case of a friend's daughter. The daughter was a very good student, but not spectacular, and graduated from a well-respected, high-performing public high school. After visiting a number of schools, public and private, she opted for Purdue University, a large public institution in West Lafayette, Indiana, that *U.S. News & World Report* ranked as No. 61 on its Best Colleges 2010 list of national universities.

If you are lucky enough to live in Indiana, Purdue is a great choice. In-state tuition for 2009-2010 was $8,638, a relatively reasonable annual investment in your future. Purdue offers more than 200 programs of study, it has an educational history that goes back 140 years, and the Boilermakers have earned eight Big Ten Conference championships in football. With attributes like that, it's easy to see why nearly 32,000 undergraduates would choose to attend

Purdue. However, for a student who lives in, say, Ohio, there might be more financially viable options. This friend and her daughter learned that for themselves, but not before eating up college savings.

For an out-of-state student, the sticker price for Purdue topped $35,000 per year – $26,000 in tuition and fees and about $9,500 in room and board. After one year at Purdue, the family decided they really couldn't afford the cost, even with all the deductions that the school had offered as enticement. The daughter ended up withdrawing from Purdue and enrolling at The Ohio State University instead, a school that ranks No. 53 on the *U.S. News* list, offers 170 majors, has more than 40,000 undergraduates, has nearly 140 years of history, and boasts 33 Big Ten Conference football championships, as well as seven national football titles. Best of all, those admirable attributes come at a much more reasonable (but still considerable) price: about $20,000 annually after grant and scholarship awards for her good grades and test scores are applied.

Size

Another important factor to consider when narrowing your list of colleges to those that best suit your needs is size of the campus. How large is the institution you're considering? How many students are enrolled? Does its size match your comfort zone?

Colleges differ dramatically in size. Public research universities are the biggest, on average, with more than 31,000 students enrolled. Arizona State University, the nation's largest public university, had an enrollment of more than 55,500 students in 2009. Regional public universities have fewer students, averaging an enrollment of about 7,000 students. Many private, not-for-profit schools range in size from about 2,000 to 5,000 students. Many are even smaller.

A smaller campus means it will be easier to learn your way around and probably much easier to find your niche. A smaller campus also means you may interact with faculty members from the day you arrive on campus. You may even have the opportunity as an undergraduate to work on research projects with faculty in your field of study. You will likely have less competition in pursuing interests in sports, student government or other extracurricular activities. Private colleges pride themselves on helping you grow as a person while you're also growing your intellectual capacity. Keeping the campus relatively small helps them to do that.

Such an intimate learning environment is not what you will find at a large public institution. One of the ways in which large research universities are able to keep costs down is that they deploy their graduate students to teach lower-level classes. That means you may not be taught by a professor holding a doctorate degree until your junior year, and maybe even later than that. Unless you're in an honors program or some other specialized curriculum, expect class sizes, particularly during your freshman and sophomore years, to be large. Classes of 200 students or more are not unusual, particularly for lower-level general education courses. At a large school, you may not get the extra help you need, or you may have to work harder to find it.

Although many bigger institutions are working harder to engage students and make their campuses feel smaller, you should assume that it will be more challenging for you to carve a niche for yourself in a supersized setting. For some students that's a daunting prospect; for others, it's not.

Selectivity

Students and parents usually think about selectivity strictly in terms of how challenging it is to get into a particular college. Beyond simply telling you how difficult or easy it will be for you to get in, a school's selectivity can also tell you what the student body makeup is likely to be. What is the average SAT or ACT score for students who are accepted? What percentage of students accepted were in the top 25 percent of their high school class? That information is valuable in understanding how well you will fit in and how difficult it may be for you to keep up with your classmates.

It's good to be challenged academically, but it's better to be in an academic environment where you have a chance to shine. If you shoot for comfortable rather than challenging, perhaps you'll be more likely to ask questions when you don't understand and contribute your insights instead of keeping them to yourself. That's more of a real opportunity for you to grow personally and academically. When we look at success rate, you can see why "fit" with the academic environment might be one of the most important things to consider.

Success Rate

Perhaps the most poorly understood factor for narrowing college choice is success rate. In simple terms, success rate is measured two ways. First, "retention rate" is the percentage of a college's freshman students who return for their sophomore year. This indicates whether a school can hold onto its students in the short run. The second measurement of a college's success is its "six-year graduation rate," which reflects the percentage of students who come in as freshmen and graduate from that school within six years. The second number tells you a lot more than the first.

Schools have dramatically different six-year graduation rates. The colleges and universities themselves would like you to think that the differences in student success have something to do with the schools themselves. That may be true in some cases, but don't be fooled. Just look at the data.

How Different Types of Universities Stack Up			
	Top 100 Research Universities (Public & Private)	Private Non-Profit Colleges & Universities	Public Colleges & Universities
Average 6-Year Graduation Rate	76%	55%	46%
Average (OLD) SAT Score (1600 scale)	1243	1079	1012
Average (NEW) SAT Score (2400 scale)	1860	1620	1525
Correlation Between 6-Year Graduation Rate & Average SAT Score	89%	82%	76%
Correlation Between 6-Year Graduation Rate & Percent of Pell Grant Recipients	-56%	-69%	-61%

In the first row of the table above, you can see the average graduation rates for three categories of colleges and universities. Column 1 shows data for the elite research universities, both public and private, in the United States. As you can see, they have the best six-year graduation rate, but they also have a very high average SAT score. The 1243 average (old) SAT score at the top 100 research universities represents about the 85th percentile. This means that, on average, students in these universities tend to be the academic all-stars. Because these schools specialize in attracting academic all-stars, it shouldn't come as any surprise that their six-year graduation rate is, on average, 76 percent, which means that three out of four of their entering freshmen graduate.

Basically, this chart tells us that the reason some schools have better graduation rates than others is mostly because they have more students who scored well on the

SAT. It doesn't tell you *anything* about how well that particular school is going to fit *your* needs.

The other thing this chart shows is that the big sticker price and intimate setting of small private colleges don't guarantee you will finish. The non-elite publics and privates have relatively similar "success" rates.

Pay attention to graduation rates when you're looking for a college, but be sure you know what you are comparing. Schools that admit students with high test scores tend to have good graduation rates. What you need to look for is whether a school is likely to be able to provide the kind of support and nurturing that *you* need to succeed.

One more thing: A 2004 report from the Pell Institute for the Study of Opportunity in Higher Education found that colleges with greater numbers of students receiving Pell Grants had lower graduation rates. Only students with lower family incomes are eligible for Pell Grants. So this tells you that people who don't have a lot of money to invest in a college education are at greater risk of not graduating. Most of the students who go to universities with high "success rates" come from families with enough financial resources to make sure their student can pay tuition, room and board. This supports what we said in earlier chapters. You need to make sure that you pay attention not only to the academics, but the price tag, as well.

Cram Session

- Four key criteria – sticker price, size, selectivity and success rate – give you the data to narrow your field of choices to colleges that best match your circumstances and needs.
- "Retention rate" is the percentage of a college's freshman students who return for their sophomore year. This indicates whether a school can hold onto its students in the short run.

- The second measurement of a college's success is its "six-year graduation rate," which reflects the percentage of students who come in as freshmen and graduate from that school within six years.
- The reason some schools have better graduation rates than others is mostly because they have more students who scored well on the SAT and ACT.
- Brand name doesn't guarantee a good undergraduate education environment for you.

Key Concepts:
business strategy
leverage
academic capital
financial capital

Chapter 9
What's Right for You? Strategies for Leveraging Your Capabilities

When business executives decide to develop a new strategy for their company, their first step is to determine what capital and capabilities the firm has to work with. One key principle of business planning is that you should match your strategy to your resources and capabilities. We think this holds true for educational planning, as well.

If you are going to find an educational strategy that makes sense for your situation, you need to think in terms of two capabilities and resources: your academic capital and your financial capital. Your educational strategy should be different based on where you fall in these two key areas. As we've already discussed, families and students don't tend to think of these things as equally important to their college decision. But we hope that we have convinced you otherwise by now.

If you buy into the idea that you need to realistically assess both types of capital, then combining these two elements reveals four basic strategies for helping you to move beyond your high school education and get on track for a successful career. To help you understand what we mean, look at the following grid. Think about where you are, high or low, on each of the two elements. Depending on how you rate yourself, you will find different options to think about. For example, if you have good test scores (high academic capital) but your family has little money saved (low financial capital), you may want to think differently about your years after high school than if you have lower test scores (low academic capital) but your family has diligently

Academic Capital

	NO	YES
YES	Strategy 3: **Leverage Financial Capital**	Strategy 1: **Grab the Brass Ring**
NO	Strategy 4: **Be Practical and Pragmatic**	Strategy 2: **Leverage Academic Capital**

(vertical label: **Financial Capital**)

Your Personal Profile

A) Do you have *more* than $50,000 in financial assets available for your educational investment (without borrowing)?   YES   NO

B) Do you have an ACT of *at least* 21 and a combined verbal and qualitative score on the SAT *greater than* 1050 OR total SAT score greater than 1500 (including writing)?   YES   NO

Strategy 1: A=Yes and B=Yes   Strategy 2: A=No and B=Yes
Strategy 3: A=Yes and B=No   Strategy 4: A=No and B=No

put money aside for you since you were born (high financial capital). In the table at the bottom of the preceding page, we offer some rough guidelines for helping you know where to put yourself on the grid, but these guidelines are only meant to give you an idea. Only you can assess your own interest and financial comfort zone.

The following four scenarios demonstrate the different strategies on the grid. If you know where you fall, you may only want to read the scenario that best matches your circumstances. But, as we have noted earlier, the recent economic turmoil should teach us all one thing: Circumstances can change dramatically in a short amount of time. You may find that the other categories give you useful advice and help prepare you for whatever changes may come your way.

Leverage Strategy 1: Grab the Brass Ring – "I love school, I'm good at it, and my parents have been saving money since I was a baby. I'm ready to go!"

If this describes your level of academic interest and financial assets, then way to go. You're one of the lucky ones. You can fo-

What This Means for You

A few years ago, the SAT underwent a series of changes. Some content was added; other content was removed. The most notable difference was the addition of a new writing section, which increased the maximum score from 1600 to 2400.

The Princeton Review has put together a chart that compares the old SAT to the new SAT in terms of content, time, cost and scores. You can find the chart at www.princetonreview.com.tw/college/chart.htm. A score of 1100 on the old test, for example, would roughly equal a score of 1650 on the new SAT.

Because many colleges have tracked to the old number, some schools only look at Math and Critical Reasoning (which used to be Verbal). Other schools look at all three sections and make a conversion to compare to past admissions decisions. Make sure you understand your score and what kind of academic leverage it might provide.

cus on maximizing your experiences instead of minimizing your hurdles. If you're smart, and apparently you are, you should already be thinking beyond a bachelor's degree to a graduate or professional degree that will help set you apart in the marketplace.

You are the traditional student for whom most college-planning books are written. You should choose the best school that fits what you want out of a college experience. Specifically, consider elite research universities, whether private or public. Understand that this level of academic success comes with a steep price tag, however. Tuition alone among elite private research institutions averages $34,965 per year, according to National Center for Education Statistics data; roll in room, board and books and the total sticker price tops $46,000 per year. This means a four-year price tag of $184,000. If you have the money, the doors that such a prestigious, brand-name experience is likely to open for you may make this a good investment.

The challenge at these top research schools is getting in: Fewer than 29 percent of students who apply to elite private research universities are accepted. Anyone with an SAT score of less than 1900 on the new scale (roughly 1260 on the old) or an ACT composite score lower than 28 shouldn't waste her or his time applying. The stellar graduation numbers at these schools stem, in part, from the fact that they are able to attract motivated, academically gifted students who tend to have financial resources to tap.

If your financial savings account isn't quite hefty enough or your SAT scores aren't high enough for an elite private school, then focus on the best public research university in your state. The price tag will likely be easier to manage. And public research universities tend to have higher acceptance rates (about 65%) because they need more students to support what is usually a much larger campus.

There is a downside to the Brass Ring Strategy. Having

so many high achievers in one setting is a mixed blessing. You may decide you like the intellectual challenge and feel that being around some of the best and the brightest serves to make you even better and brighter than you already are. Some students, however, don't like the stress of the constant high-stakes academic competition. If you fall into that category, this type of school environment may not be right for you, even if you get accepted and can afford it.

For those of you with academic aptitude and financial assets, there is one more thing to consider. You might be better off saving your money on the undergraduate degree and putting those resources toward graduate school. For people with the talent, means and inclination, graduate school is how they can set themselves apart from the growing number of people with bachelor's degrees. Remember, in general, more education leads to a higher paycheck. In 2008, according to Current Population Survey data, workers with a master's degree earned $221 more per week, on average, than workers with only a bachelor's degree. Workers with a professional or doctorate degree earned about $500 more per week than those with a bachelor's degree. But that extra education is going to cost you. *Don't make the mistake of overspending on your bachelor's degree if your plan is to go on to other educational endeavors.*

Leverage Strategy 2: Leverage Academic Capital – "I love school and I'm good at it, but there's no way my family can afford this."

If this is you, don't fret. You really do have good options. And the better the student you are, the more options you have. Your best strategy is to leverage your academic aptitude to cover your lack of financial assets. If you are an exceptionally good student, with SAT scores above 2100 on the new scale (about 1400 on the old) or an ACT score of 31 or so, stellar grades and compelling personal experiences, you may be able to access the most rarefied air of a private research university without the high cost. For example, in 2008, Harvard University announced that it would allow students from middle-income families who were accepted to attend school tuition free. In the competitive game to attract the best and the brightest, many other elite, highly selective schools followed suit. However, many of these schools saw their endowments shrink dramatically during the financial crisis so this great generosity may be short-lived.

If you are lucky enough to have extraordinary academic talent that shows up on the SAT or ACT score, or if you have some other gift such as music or athletics, many schools will track you down and try to give you money. This is what we mean by leveraging your academic assets. You should work to convert those special skills and aptitudes into enough financial discounts (scholarships and grants) to cover most of the cost of your college. *If you do need to supplement your scholarships with student loans, you need to remember to keep them, in total, to no more than you would be willing to pay for a car.*

Because you don't have much money on hand to cover the costs of college, you want to cast your net wide and get as many offers as you can. (One caveat here is that many schools charge a fee simply to apply. You can sometimes get around the fee by applying online or by demonstrating financial hardship.) By having a strong academic portfolio, you might be able to score more money from public and private universities that *aren't* among the elite 100 universities. With so many colleges chasing top students, you are in an advantageous position to negotiate a good deal, especially among lower-tiered schools. Don't be afraid to entertain multiple offers and let each school know that it needs to put forth its best deal if it wants to get your attention.

If you really enjoy school but, for whatever reason, your SAT or ACT score is only in the respectable range, you can incorporate some of the strategies in Chapter 6 to bring your costs down. Your biggest challenge is going to be avoiding too much debt. Your best approach might be to target public regional campuses in your area. A lot of public regional universities really appreciate "good," hardworking students and are willing to provide as much support as they can afford. They might not be able to give you a full scholarship, but they might be willing to help you out with work study or other financial support.

Regional public universities are usually much less expensive, but they still can provide you with a strong undergraduate education. If you are a good student and excel in this more modest environment, you might benefit from the "big fish/small pond" effect. Your chances to make friends of faculty and alumni are much better. You also may be surprised that many of these schools have top-notch faculty who may have been trained at top-tier schools. With smaller "academic capital" to leverage, it will go further in an environment that really appreciates it. Many regional schools that know they can't go after the academic cream of the crop like to target the next level of talent where the competition isn't so stiff.

If your SAT and ACT scores put you closer to the 50th percentile, your odds of success are still good – especially on a regional public or very small private campus. If you aren't in the money because of your academic background, see if you can leverage a hobby or some other personal talent into financial backing. Sometimes picking a major in an area with fewer students can give you access to scholarships put aside only for students with specific profiles. For example, women and minority students interested in studying science, technology or engineering are sometimes able to get financial support. Teaching is another area with financial opportunity. If you offer to teach in high-need or low-income urban and rural areas after graduation, you can afford to take out more student loans because much of your debt may be forgiven after a certain number of years of service. Because you are starting with less financial capital, you may have to work a little harder and be a bit more creative to turn your academic capability into a financial resource. But opportunities are out there if you really take the time to look.

Leverage Strategy 3: Leverage Financial Capital – "School is not my thing, but my parents have been saving for this all my life. I dread another four years!"

If this describes you, then your financial capital tops your academic capital. You need to figure out how to keep your academic weaknesses from getting in the way of your career success. You actually have more options than you probably think. The good news is that your parents have a pot of money that you can access. More good news is that college isn't like high school. You won't see the same instructor day after day; you won't have nearly as many confining rules. But, on the other hand, college is much more self-directed. You won't have somebody after you every day to get your work done, and you will largely have to figure out for yourself how to function within the system.

If your less-than-stellar grades were your way of rebelling against a confining high school system that failed to make learning seem relevant to you, you may be surprised. You may find that college gives you the opportunities to explore interests that you never had before. That's the wonderful, amazing potential of the college experience. It truly can be a transformative, defining time in students' lives. But, don't kid yourself, you'll have to work for it. And if you've slacked off and barely gotten through high school, you really lack the good academic practices – paying attention in class, completing all your homework, keeping up on reading assignments – to succeed. College success boils down to aptitude *and* attitude. Poor aptitude or poor attitude, either one, can hold you back.

If the idea of four – or, more likely, five or six – more years of school turns you off because you struggled with the content and workload in high school, you have different issues but you still have options. Find the right college program that matches your needs and interests, and you may be surprised at what you're capable of. This is where the idea of "fit" that many college planners preach really pays off.

Whether your difficulties with high school stemmed from attitude or aptitude, you will need to look for schools that are less selective. Don't waste your time fantasizing about getting into the "best" schools because it won't happen – unless, of course, your parents have financed a building on campus. When there's that kind of money in play, anything can happen. But, even if you were to get into one of the elite schools, you likely wouldn't be able to keep up with the highly motivated, high-achieving students on those campuses. Such a highly charged, rigorous environment won't serve you well.

If you can truly afford it, begin your search by focusing on colleges that place greater importance on teaching than research. In particular, look for private schools that emphasize student support. This is your best bet for achieving true college success – graduating.

Don't underestimate how much size matters, especially if you are a student who struggles. The small, nurturing environment of private schools allows them to focus more on individual students. You may find yourself lost at a big public institution where freshman classes for core curriculum requirements may consist of hundreds of students. Even though many public institutions are doing more to provide students with extra help if needed, that one-on-one interaction is part of the package at smaller private schools.

By now, you're probably thinking to yourself: "Ugh! I'm just going to have to suffer through another four years." Well, if it's that distasteful to you, at least the unpleasantness may give you incentive to buckle down and get through in four years instead of prolonging the agony (either yours or your parents', who are presumably funding a good piece of this torture). That's not likely, however.

Our hunch is that you will get to college and find that you actually like it. Maybe not the classwork, but you'll probably like the atmosphere. What's not to like about getting to make your own rules, come and go when you like, eat as much pizza as you want, and send the bulk of the bill to Mom and Dad? You wouldn't be the first student to want to hide out as long as possible in this idyllic setting. One young college graduate was overheard telling another: "Do you think we'll ever have as much fun as the four (or six or eight) years we spent in college?" Many college-educated adults would probably look back and ask the same question. Will we ever get to have as much fun again?

If you scored around 1500 or below on the SAT (roughly 1000 on the old test), you weren't in the top 30 percent of your graduating class and you're looking for an educational bargain, your best bet may be a regional public institution. In your own state, of course. Many of these schools focus more of their attention on undergraduates. At more research-oriented universities, teaching undergraduates often takes a back seat to performing research and conferring graduate degrees. If you struggle, you may find more help in schools that place greater emphasis on teaching.

Here's a shocking strategy for you, one we can barely bring ourselves to suggest: If you are financially prepared but you are academically challenged, look for the easiest path to a college degree that your money can buy. That means a school with low selectivity and a program with limited rigor. Preferably, pick a course of study that does offer some marketable skill set. As much as we hate to say it, among students who struggle, the most important aspect of the college experience is getting to the finish line. Get the degree. Period. It's not about the experience or the journey. *The experience without the degree gets you nowhere. The degree without the experience can still pay off.*

Leverage Strategy 4: Be Practical and Pragmatic – "I have no money and I'm not a great student. I still want to go to college. Is it hopeless?"

We hate to say it, but you are in a vulnerable spot. That doesn't mean you throw up your hands and accept a fate of low-wage, dead-end jobs. Students in your position, with little academic capital or financial capital, are the most vulnerable and the most poorly served by the current advice that every student should go to college. If you lack both the necessary knowledge and the financial resources, you are ill-prepared – and unsuited – for the typical four-year college program. If you don't want to think about college at all, then skip ahead to Chapter 12. We detail some strategies there for people who have no interest in spending another four years in higher education.

But let's say that you are a pragmatist. You don't want to go, but you realize that without a four-year degree, your options are limited. Trust us, there are more of you out there than you may think. *In your circumstances, you need education and training options that are heavy on marketable skills, quick on delivery and light on contemplating the human condition.* The Practical, Pragmatic Strategy is based on the idea that, regardless of financial capital or academic capital, success in the 21st century means some form of education after high school.

If you have struggled to make decent grades in high school, it won't be easy to make the transition to college. Here's the troubling news: High school performance tends to indicate how well you are likely to do in college.

Strategy Tip

A Pell Institute report identified colleges and universities that appeared to be succeeding in educating low-income students. The report found several common differences among the schools with high graduation rates. These better-performing schools had:

- "Intrusive" advising and periodic reviews for students who were struggling academically.
- Small classes, even for freshmen.
- Special support programs, particularly for at-risk students.
- Dedicated faculty, most engaged in teaching full time.
- Tutoring, supplemental instruction and "mastery" classes.
- Developmental and remedial education.
- Geographic isolation. (Most of the succeeding schools were found to be in rural areas or small towns, which apparently strengthened the bond between student and campus.)
- Residential requirement for freshmen.
- Shared values, whether it was small-town backgrounds, religious beliefs or racial or ethnic heritage. Five of the schools identified as having higher than average graduation rates were historically black colleges or universities.
- A real concern with retention.

Listed above are the kinds of attributes you need to look for when you are evaluating your college plans. An average ACT score of 18 or SAT score of about 1325 on the new test (or 885 on the old) will get you into these kinds of schools.

It doesn't mean you can't succeed, but the odds are not in your favor. If you are from a family without much money, you face even greater challenges. Understanding the odds from the beginning and taking steps to improve them must be central to your college search.

Although you may think your best option is to pursue the traditional four-year degree, you might actually be happier with the more pragmatic choice – your local community college. It's important for you to understand that community colleges are really interested in students just like you. Community colleges have tended to provide students an "open door" to education. They are better-positioned to serve students who need some "catch-up" help in English, math and science. Two years at a community college is also much cheaper than two years at a traditional four-year school, and states are getting better about insisting that credits earned at community college transfer easily to public four-year schools. *Earning a two-year associate's degree from a community college is a cost-effective option for transitioning from high school to the four-year bachelor's degree.* Many students may find that a two-year degree, or even a certificate program, provides them all the after-high-school education they need and more quickly allows them to gain the marketable skills to get started on their career.

Colleges That Fit the Strategies

There are thousands of public and private colleges and universities in the United States. We can't evaluate each one specifically for your needs. What we hope, though, is to provide some tools and understanding that will help you narrow the choices and target the schools that might work best for your personal situation. Not everyone has the same academic capital or the same financial capital. Even among students who fall into the same broad category of financial and academic preparation, there are individual differences.

The fact that these two elements vary so much from family to family and student to student is why you can't take a one-size-fits-all approach to the college decision. Every year families waste money, time and energy applying to colleges and universities that don't fit with their student's academic and financial profile. Every year hopes are crushed, and students feel humiliated when a school doesn't "pick" them. But consider this your chance to turn the tables. Resolve to choose your college path based on your needs, your interests and a thoughtful assessment of your circumstances. Leverage your capital in ways that are going to benefit you the most in the long run. Leverage your capital in ways that will improve the odds that you make it to graduation. Change the way this game is played, and it might just increase your odds of winning.

Cram Session

- College is not "one size fits all."
- Fewer than 29 percent of students who apply to elite private research universities are accepted.
- Regional universities and community colleges can give you a good value for the money.
- Don't underestimate how much size matters, especially if you are a student who struggles.
- Assess your financial capital as well as your academic capital.
- Don't spend all of your financial capital on your undergraduate degree. Keep some in reserve for graduate school.
- A graduate degree is how people with the talent, means and inclination can set themselves apart from the growing number of people with bachelor's degrees.

Key Concepts:
options valuation
decision matrix
weighting

Chapter 10
Putting It All Together:
Weighing Your College Options

In Chapter 8, we gave you some ideas about how colleges are different. In Chapter 9, we hope you got some insight into what types of schools might fit with your resources and capabilities. What we want to do in this chapter is put some of these ideas together to help you identify choices that match your circumstances. Remember, you want to focus on three basic goals:

1) Finding a college that appeals to your interests, fits your aptitude and improves your marketability.

2) Choosing a school that fits your family's financial resources and minimizes costs.

3) Making sure that you increase the odds that you finish and get the degree.

What Are YOUR Options?

You may have a lot of friends who are interested in a wide variety of colleges and universities. The temptation is to follow the crowd. Sometimes, it is uncomfortable to walk on your own path. What you need to remember, though, is that while you may share a high school experience, you probably won't be sharing your entire life with these same people. Everyone's circumstances are different. So if picking a college means figuring out what is right for *you* and *your* circumstances, it stands to reason that just following the crowd isn't necessarily going to result in the best solution for you.

In business, when a company has to make a decision, managers may employ a technique called Real Options Valuation, or ROV for short. ROV means that the decision-maker identifies all of the important pieces of information and assumptions that are relevant to the decision and uses certain evaluation techniques to make choices. ROV doesn't have to be limited to the business world. We can take some of those strategies and adapt them to help you and your family make the decision about college.

In this chapter, we will guide you through a process to help you identify and evaluate your college investment options. In other words, it's your COV – College Options Valuation. This information, together with the financial analysis techniques that we showed you earlier, should give you the tools you need to have a very clear idea of the set of schools that match your individual situation. Although the final choice is up to you, we hope that this exercise will guide you and empower you to make the best decision for *you.*

Getting the Information You Need

There are lots of websites you can use to get information about all the possible colleges and universities that are out there. The website we recommend is called College Navigator. Not only does the site have information on just about every kind of college (two-year, four-year, public, private) you might think of, but the information is *free!*

This database comes from good old Uncle Sam. Colleges and universities are required to report information to the federal government every year. And they have to tell the truth in their reporting. So this isn't the "marketing" packet; these data offer a real-world snapshot. We have drawn extensively on this data from the National Center for Education Statistics throughout the book.

The following steps walk you through the website so that you know how to find the information you need to compare your colleges of interest. We will show you screenshots of where to go and how to find the data you need. In Chapter 8, we identified the four key pieces of information to help you make your college decision: *sticker price, size, selectivity* and *success rate.* You can find all of this information easily through the College Navigator.

Step 1: Find the College Navigator web page.

The website for the College Navigator is:

http://nces.ed.gov/collegenavigator.

(WARNING: Don't confuse the College Navigator government website with THE COLLEGE NAVIGATOR.COM, which is a company that may charge you money for some of this very same information.)

Step 2: Identify your options.

There are several ways you can find schools using the College Navigator. One way to start is just to type in the names of the colleges or universities you are interested in. You can make your list bigger with a few clicks of your mouse. One option is to click on **Use Map**, which brings up a map of the United States. You can click on the states where you might have some interest in attending college. If, instead, you want to look relatively close to home, just enter your ZIP Code and, in the drop-down menu, pick how close you might want to be.

At this point, you might want to go ahead and click **Show Results**. But if you want to narrow the list a little more, click the **Level of Award** box. If you're sure you want a four-year degree, click **Bachelor's**. If you think that you really

Getting Started on the College Navigator

want to start at a community or technical college, click **Certificate** or **Associate**. One really nice feature of this website is that it has such a broad list of schools connected to it.

Step 3: Pull out a subgroup of the list that you generate to look at more thoroughly.

As an example, we are going to look at schools that are

Picking Some College Possibilities

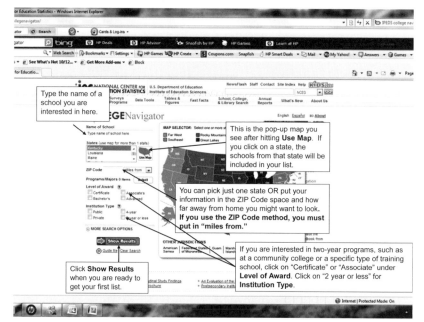

close to our hometown in Kentucky. When we were young (back in B.C. – before computers), these were some of the colleges and universities that we would have considered. To create a subgroup from the larger list, click on the box to the right of the name of the college or university to **Add to Favorites.** If you have never heard of the school before, you can roll your mouse over the circle with the lowercase "i" next to its name to get background information.

Step 4: Create a list of favorites.

After you have pulled together a list of schools that, for whatever reason, interest you, you will want to compare them. To do this, go to the **My Favorites** tab. The drop-down menu gives you the choice of clicking on the box next to the name of each school you want to compare or you can simply click **Check All**. When you have your list identified, click **Compare**.

Creating a List of Favorites

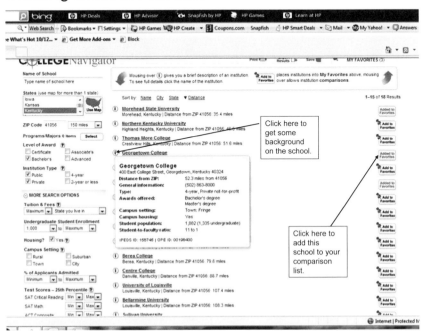

Comparing Your Favorites

Step 5: Find the four S's: Sticker Price, Size, Selectivity and Success Rate.

In our example, we have picked four Kentucky schools; two are public and two are private. Clicking on **Compare** will give us a really good idea of how much each costs, how many students are enrolled, what the SAT expectations are, and what the graduation and retention rates are for each campus. The nice thing about the College Navigator data is that not only can you get information about the sticker price, you can also get an idea of how much it is going to cost for four years of tuition. (Or two years for community colleges.)

You can find that information on the **Financial Aid** tab. The **Enrollment** tab gives you the number of students enrolled at each school. Clicking on the **Admissions** tab will show you what the SAT and ACT scores are for students at each school. **Retention and graduation rates** give you the percentage of students who graduate. *Taken together, this*

Accessing Sticker Price Data

is all the information you need to determine if any of these schools might work for you.

On the next two screenshots, you can see what each college will cost each year and what four years of tuition will cost for each institution. You can get the total cost for a year by clicking on **Estimated Student Expenses (Before Aid).** You can find the four-year tuition total by clicking on the **Calculate Tuition** button.

The sticker price for four years is going to look pretty high. Luckily, you can also find out the average amount of financial aid each school offers. After accounting for the amount that students tend to get in grants, scholarships and *student* (not parent) loans, you can see how much money the average family is going to have to contribute each year in the **Net Price** section. This section provides a pretty realistic idea about the amount of money that you and your family will have to come up with each year. The information presented is based on in-state tuition and is

Estimating Student Expenses for One Year

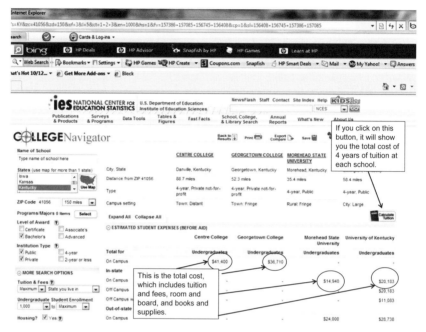

Calculating Tuition for Four Years

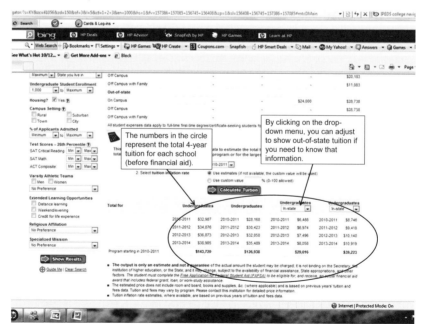

Getting a Sense of Your Bottom-Line Investment

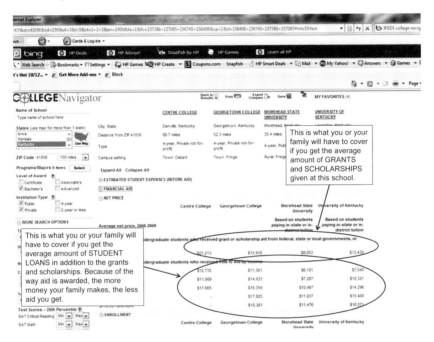

shown by estimated family income. Don't forget to multiply the number by four to get the total expected bottom line for your entire investment. Given that so many students take longer than four years, you should multiply by five or even six so that you know what delaying graduation will cost you. If you don't live in the state where the *public* institution is located, don't forget to adjust for out-of-state tuition. This will give you the **Sticker Price.**

The next piece of information you want to pull is **Size**. Size is important because some people really perform better in a smaller environment. You probably don't really know what size campus is right for you. Large means a greater variety of activities, maybe better sports teams, maybe a larger city. But it also usually means that it's harder to get to know people, that classes may be larger (especially for freshmen), and that you can get lost in the crowd. To get a sense of what the campus size is for each school of interest, click on **Enrollment** to see information about campus demographics.

Sizing Up Your List of Favorites

The table shown in the screenshot:

	Centre College	Georgetown College	Morehead State University	University of Kentucky
Total enrollment	1,216	1,882	8,822	26,295
Undergraduate enrollment	1,216	1,335	7,326	19,183
Undergraduate transfer-in enrollment	8	38	426	1,234
Undergraduates by Attendance Status				
Full-time	100%	96%	76%	
Part-time	0%	4%	24%	
Undergraduates by Gender				
Male	45%	44%	39%	
Female	55%	56%	61%	
Undergraduates by Race / ethnicity				
American Indian or Alaska Native	0%	0%	0%	
Asian/Native Hawaiian/Pacific Islander	3%	0%	0%	2%
Black or African American	4%	7%	3%	7%
Hispanic/Latino	2%	1%	1%	2%
White	88%	90%	93%	85%
Two or more races	0%	0%	0%	0%
Race/ethnicity unknown	0%	0%	2%	3%
Non-resident alien	2%	1%	0%	1%
Undergraduates by Age				
24 and under	100%	98%	75%	90%

Callout box: "Here is the information on campus size. But, as you can see, there is a lot more you can find out."

Selectivity data are found in the **Admissions** section of the College Navigator. For our purposes, selectivity has to do with how well the students at each university scored on the SAT and ACT college admissions exams. Although we agree with test critics that this doesn't completely show your academic readiness, test scores do give you an idea of how stiff the competition sitting next to you in class might be.

The College Navigator shows the SAT and ACT scores for the bottom 25 percent (25th percentile) and the top 25 percent (75th percentile) of students in the entering freshman class. If your score is *higher* than the bottom 25 percent, you would probably do fine in most classrooms and programs at the school you are considering. If your score is lower than that, then you should think about whether that school is going to be a good fit for you. If your score is *above* the 75th percentile, you should do well in this school and you might be eligible for academic scholarship money.

Understanding How Selective Your Choices Are

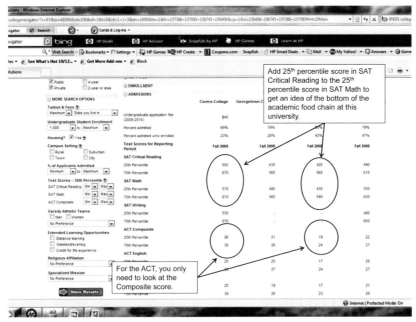

The data in the College Navigator are divided into the components of each admissions test. For the SAT, you should add the two main components (Critical Reading and Math) to get the total score that most schools consider. For the ACT, look at the composite score to decide whether you would likely feel comfortable in this university's classrooms. Why should you care about this? If you are in the bottom 25 percent in the university, your odds of leaving without your degree go way up. Remember, one of the primary goals is to improve your odds of graduation!

OK, now we are ready for the final piece, **Success Rate**. We encourage you to look at the university success rate, but, in reality, the only success rate you *really* should care about is your own. Success rate indicates how many freshmen who entered the school together actually graduated. Usually, you should look at the six-year graduation rate. If 100 freshmen entered in Year 1, how many graduated six years later? Ideally, this number would be high, but there

Assessing How Likely You Are to Graduate

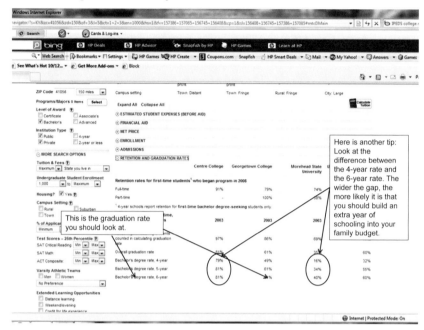

This is the graduation rate you should look at.

Here is another tip: Look at the difference between the 4-year rate and the 6-year rate. The wider the gap, the more likely it is that you should build an extra year of schooling into your family budget.

Saving Your Comparisons

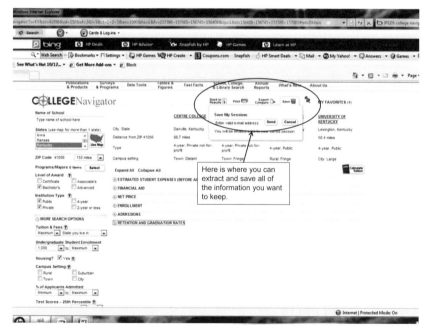

Here is where you can extract and save all of the information you want to keep.

are a *lot* of things that derail graduation plans. We talked about some of those issues back in Chapter 9. You do want to know this number, though, because if you are looking at two schools with similar selectivity and sticker price, then the one with the higher success rate might be the better option for you. Think of this information as sort of a tiebreaker.

At any time you can save all of this information by clicking on **Print** for a hard copy, **Export** to dump the information into an Excel spreadsheet, or **Save** to have a link to the information sent to your e-mail account.

Using the Information to Help With the College Decision

You can just "eyeball" the information you have collected and get a sense of what might suit you and your parents, or you can go one step further and actually systematically evaluate the information using a business tool called a Decision Matrix. The value of taking this one further step is that it allows you to have a more productive conversation with your parents about the trade-offs of various choices and helps you be clear about why you might favor one college over another.

We created worksheets to help you do your own analysis. They are in a separate chapter at the end of this book. Here, we'll walk through how the Decision Matrix works.

We said that it is important to look at selectivity, sticker price, size and success rate. In this example, we have a hypothetical student, Samantha, who has an SAT score of 1000 and who is comparing the four colleges we mentioned earlier on the four key pieces of information that we pulled from College Navigator. We recorded the information in a Decision Matrix that looks like this:

Name of School	Do you have the Academic Capital? SELECTIVITY		Do you have the Financial Capital? STICKER PRICE		How big is your campus comfort zone? SIZE		Does the school get people through? SUCCESS RATE		SCORE
	Average of the 25th and 75th percentile score (A)	Rank based on how close to your score	Net sticker price based on family income	Rank based on net sticker price (B)	Student enrollment	Rank based on student enrollment (C)	6-year graduation rate	Rank based on 6-year graduation rate (D)	Unweighted score (A+B+C+D)
Centre College	1230		$17,665		1,216		81%		
Georgetown College	1015		$16,354		1,882		61%		
Morehead State University	1000		$10,497		8,822		40%		
University of Kentucky	1115		$14,296		26,295		60%		

(A) The school score that is closest to your score should be ranked No. 1. The school that is furthest from your score should be ranked No. 4.

(B) The school with the lowest sticker price should be ranked No. 1. The school with the highest sticker price should be ranked No. 4.

(C) If you prefer LARGE schools, the school with the largest enrollment should be ranked No. 1 and the smallest ranked No. 4. If you prefer SMALL schools, then the school with the smallest enrollment should be ranked No. 1, and the school with the largest should be ranked No. 4.

(D) The school with the highest graduation rate should be ranked No. 1. The school with the lowest graduation rate should be ranked No. 4.

All of these pieces of information are quite different. That means we need some way to make it easy to combine all these elements so that we can see how the schools stack up. There are several ways to do this, but the easiest technique is ranking. On the next page, you will find an example of how Samantha might get started.

We are going to have Samantha rank each school on each of the four pieces of information. To keep it simple, for each piece of data, the school that is *closest* to her individual profile is ranked No. 1. The school that is *furthest* from her personal profile is ranked No. 4 (because we only have four schools). For example, of the four schools, the one with the average SAT score closest to her score was ranked No. 1, and the school with the SAT average furthest from her score was ranked No. 4.

Because Samantha comes from a middle-income family, the least expensive school was ranked No. 1 (because she worries about money), and the most expensive was ranked No. 4. Samantha is ready to move from her small hometown and likes the idea of a big school; therefore, the biggest school was ranked No. 1, and the smallest was ranked No. 4. Finally, the school with the best graduation rate was ranked No. 1, and the worst was ranked No. 4. (That's not her opinion; that is always the case.)

After Samantha ranked the schools based on how the information matched her circumstances, she could then total the score for each school. The school with the lowest score (remember, we ranked our schools with the lowest number being the best) should offer the best fit for our young friend. In this case, that would be Morehead State University.

On the next page, you can see how Samantha ranked each school for the four different categories. You can also see that Morehead ends up with the lowest score, just ahead of the University of Kentucky.

Let's assume, for the sake of argument, that Samantha

Name of School	Do you have the Academic Capital? SELECTIVITY		Do you have the Financial Capital? STICKER PRICE		How big is your campus comfort zone? SIZE		Does the school get people through? SUCCESS RATE		SCORE
	Average of the 25th and 75th percentile score (A)	Rank based on how close to your score (A)	Net sticker price based on family income (B)	Rank based on net sticker price (B)	Student enrollment	Rank based on student enrollment (C)	6-year graduation rate	Rank based on 6-year graduation rate (D)	Unweighted score (A+B+C+D)
Centre College	1230	4	$17,665	4	1,216	4	81%	1	13
Georgetown College	1015	2	$16,354	3	1,882	3	61%	2	10
Morehead State University	1000	1	$10,497	1	8,822	2	40%	4	8
University of Kentucky	1115	3	$14,296	2	26,295	1	60%	3	9

(A) The school score that is closest to your score should be ranked No. 1. The school that is furthest from your score should be ranked No. 4.

(B) The school with the lowest sticker price should be ranked No. 1. The school with the highest sticker price should be ranked No. 4.

(C) If you prefer LARGE schools, the school with the largest enrollment should be ranked No. 1 and the smallest ranked No. 4. If you prefer SMALL schools, then the school with the smallest enrollment should be ranked No. 1, and the school with the largest should be ranked No. 4.

(D) The school with the highest graduation rate should be ranked No. 1. The school with the lowest graduation rate should be ranked No. 4.

would prefer the bright lights and basketball of the University of Kentucky in Lexington rather than the rolling hills of the state's rural eastern region. Our student friend would like to see if she could present a case to her parents that the larger school would be a better fit than the smaller one. In that case, adding "weights" or "priorities" to the analysis would be useful.

To add "weights," she would need to think in terms of how she might distribute 100 priority points across the four pieces of information. The piece of information most important to her would get the highest number of priority points, and the piece of information least important to her would get the lowest number of priority points. Divided across the four pieces of information, the priority points must add up to 100. The Decision Matrix that she would need to fill out appears at right.

Name of the School	Do you have the Academic Capital? SELECTIVITY			Do you have the Financial Capital? STICKER PRICE			How big is your campus comfort zone? SIZE			Does the school get people through? SUCCESS RATE			SCORE
	Average of the 25th and 75th percentile	Rank based on how close to your score	(A) Weight: How important to you? ___ points*	Net sticker price based on family income	Rank based on net sticker price	(B) Weight: How important to you? ___ points*	Student enrollment	Rank based on student enrollment	(C) Weight: How important to you? ___ points*	6-year graduation rate	Rank based on 6-year graduation rate	(D) Weight: How important to you? ___ points*	Weighted score (A+B+C+D)
Centre College	1230	4		$17,665	4		1,216	4		81%	1		
Georgetown College	1015	2		$16,354	3		1,882	3		61%	2		
Morehead State University	1000	1		$10,497	1		8,822	2		40%	4		
University of Kentucky	1115	3		$14,296	2		26,295	1		60%	3		

*Only you know how important each category is to you. Try dividing 100 points among the four categories. If you're really focused on cost, you might give that category 50 points. If you don't care about size, you might give that category only 10 points. You might give success rate 25 and selectivity 15. Then multiply the weight you gave each category by the rank for each of the four schools.

Name of the School	Do you have the Academic Capital? SELECTIVITY			Do you have the Financial Capital? STICKER PRICE			How big is your campus comfort zone? SIZE			Does the school get people through? SUCCESS RATE			SCORE
	Average of the 25th and 75th percentile	Rank based on how close to your score	(A) Weight: How important to you? 20 points*	Net sticker price based on family income	Rank based on net sticker price	(B) Weight: How important to you? 20 points*	Student enrollment	Rank based on student enrollment	(C) Weight: How important to you? 50 points*	6-year graduation rate	Rank based on 6-year graduation rate	(D) Weight: How important to you? 10 points*	Weighted score (A+B+C+D)
Centre College	1230	4	80	$17,665	4	80	1,216	4	200	81%	1	10	370
Georgetown College	1015	2	40	$16,354	3	60	1,882	3	150	61%	2	20	270
Morehead State University	1000	1	20	$10,497	1	20	8,822	2	100	40%	4	40	180
University of Kentucky	1115	3	60	$14,296	2	40	26,295	1	50	60%	3	30	180

*Only you know how important each category is to you. Try dividing 100 points among the four categories. If you're really focused on cost, you might give that category 50 points. If you don't care about size, you might give that category only 10 points. You might give success rate 25 and selectivity 15. Then multiply the weight you gave each category by the rank for each of the four schools.

To recalculate the final score for each school, Samantha would need to multiply the rank times the number of priority points for each piece of information and for each school option.

At left is what Samantha's Decision Matrix would look like based on the idea that her most important consideration was university size (and basketball). In order to convince her parents that the University of Kentucky would be the right place to go, she gave 50 of her 100 priority points to that one piece of information, hoping that, in the end, her new weighted score would point in that direction.

As you can see, even with placing huge weight on wanting to go to a bigger school, Morehead State University still ended up tied with the University of Kentucky as offering Samantha the best fit. This is because, at the end of the day, Morehead State ranked No. 1 or No. 2 on three of the four pieces of data. The only piece of data for which it had a lower rank was success rate, and our friend gave that criterion only 10 priority points out of the 100 possible. Now, we wish she would have paid more attention to our earlier discussion about the importance of graduating, but perhaps she figured that being at a bigger, more exciting campus would keep her engaged in the educational process.

Our friend may indeed be able to convince her parents that the University of Kentucky is the best choice for her, but, after working through these steps, everyone would be able to see what the choice was based on. At the very least, Samantha may be more motivated to make sure that her college investment pays off because of the extra $16,000 ($4,000 difference in annual price times four years) that she and her parents will have to scrape up to send her there.

The Decision Matrix isn't a magic answer machine for college choice, but it does give you a way to think through the decision and think through your priorities. You can revise the Decision Matrix by adding more data. Certainly, if you put more colleges into the mix, you are not as likely to get such a clear-cut answer as you will with only four schools. But it is a helpful tool because it takes a lot of information and a lot of options and gives you a way to make sense of them all.

Part THREE:
Not-So-Radical Final Thoughts

Key Concepts:
know-how
co-operative education
service learning
knowledge flow

Chapter 11
Improving Your Job Odds:
Know-How vs. Know-What

Earlier, we discussed how the college decision is different in the 21st century. Now we want to add one more element for you to consider when you think about the big picture of how college will prepare you for entry into the world of work. "What" you learn at college has always been important, but in today's marketplace, it's only part of the picture. In an economy that rewards knowledge, it's not just "know-what" that will get you employed and help keep you that way. It's "know-how."

Here's a true story that illustrates the difference between "know-what" and "know-how." Picture a precocious 11-year-old boy walking the midway of carny games at a county fair, the $10 he had just earned by mowing his grandmother's yard burning a hole in his pocket. After sizing up the assortment of games offered, he stops to study one booth promising stuffed animals bigger than the boy himself to anyone who can take one shot at pool, successfully calling which ball would go in which hole.

"I think I'm going to try that," he says, after a few more minutes of study.

"But you don't play pool," says his much-wiser-to-the-ways-of-the-world mother, sure that $2 is about to be instantly lost.

"Why, Mother," he says, with an air of certainty that comes from not knowing how much he doesn't know. "It's a simple matter of physics and geometry."

So he plunks down his hard-earned money, confident that his knowledge will bring him success. He walks carefully around the table, lines up his shot – red ball in the corner pocket – and taps the cue ball feebly. The white ball wobbles slowly across the table, missing the targeted red ball entirely but nudging another toward the opposite corner. Wrong ball, wrong hole, wrong path.

The game operator, seeing no others willing to part with their money so eagerly, kindly lets the boy have another try. Then another. And another. After nearly a dozen tries, the boy finally manages to apply those "simple" principles of physics and geometry well enough to get the red ball to drop into a hole. The carny, probably giving little thought to physics theories or geometric equations but relying on the expertise that comes from practice, then deftly clears the table of the remaining balls.

"Now that, my dear," says the mother, "is the difference between theory and application."

Or, in other words, the difference between knowing what to do versus knowing how to do it. That, in a nutshell, is why pundits and advisers are wrong when they throw out the term "knowledge economy" and suggest that just amassing more and more knowledge will be enough for you to get ahead. If you want to win at the game of life, grab the brass ring, make it to the corner office or simply win a supersized stuffed dog, you need know-how.

How the Internet Challenges Higher Education

Before the 21st century ushered in rapid technological changes and worldwide access to information, colleges and universities were where people had to go to acquire valuable knowledge from the experts – professors.

Simply knowing more helped set college graduates apart from less-educated competitors looking to land a job or move up in a company. Before the Internet, when acquiring information took a lot more effort (think about those before-computer days when people actually looked things up in books and had to search the index or read the whole book to even figure out if it mentioned the topic they were interested in), people who were blessed with "knowing lots of stuff" had a competitive advantage in the workplace over those who didn't.

But any of us with access to the Internet can now quickly tap into more collective knowledge than we can ever possibly use. You've probably heard the saying that "two heads are better than one." Multiply that by millions, and you can see the power of the Internet in allowing us all to tap vast stores of knowledge, almost instantly. Enabled by the Internet, any of us can acquire information from a variety of sources. Colleges and universities no longer control access to the supply of knowledge.

So what, you may be asking yourself, does any of this have to do with choosing a college and finding a job? Plenty.

A traditional four-year college deals a lot more with "know-what" than "know-how." While the "know-what" you learn in college provides a good foundation for your future, that alone doesn't enhance your chances in the job market. The workplace has changed dramatically over the past couple of decades, but undergraduate higher education hasn't really changed to keep pace. Too many colleges are stuck in their traditional role of delivering "know-what." But the knowledge economy doesn't simply reward "know-what." Instead, it rewards how skillfully and productively you can put the knowledge that you do have to use. *The employees with a workplace advantage are the ones who know what to do with the knowledge they have acquired and can apply what they learn. In other words, the ones with "know-how."*

Know How to What?

That's a good question. As we demonstrated earlier in the book, not all knowledge is valued equally in the marketplace, even in a so-called "knowledge economy." We've already mentioned some specific jobs and fields that are expected to be in demand over the next decade or so. Scanning the Occupational Outlook Handbook or perusing any number of articles and resources about career projections can give you a sense of specific skills that may be prized in the marketplace. However, the marketplace is changing at lightning speed. Many of today's hot jobs weren't even heard of a decade or two ago. Plus, projections are simply educated guesses. There are no guarantees that specific jobs will be out there by the time you graduate and are ready to enter the workforce.

Several occupations that the OOH projected to be among the fastest-growing through 2016 didn't appear on the updated list for 2018. So, instead of trying to anticipate particular occupational know-how that will give you an advantage in the workplace of years from now, we encourage you to look for ways to gain the combination of knowledge and skills that will enable you to be the kind of adaptive worker employers crave. In particular, today's employers say they want workers who know how to learn, know how to work with others and know how to share their knowledge.

Know How to Learn

College courses and experiences that create some curiosity, some fire within, are critical to creating the skill sets associated with learning. This is one reason why, even though you need to keep an eye on the market value of your degree, you need to find something during your college career that really captures your imagination. Imagination and curiosity drive the desire to learn. Searching, experimenting, combining things in new and different ways develop the critical-thinking skills that employers want to see. The sense of satisfaction that comes from finding a creative solution or going beyond expectations will stay with you forever. Being open to new learning (this comes to some people naturally; others have to work on it the same way they work on other skills) will allow you continually to refresh your knowledge base and your skill set, keeping you employable long after your undergraduate degree has become dated or even obsolete.

Know How to Work With Others

A reality of the working world is the need to work in groups and teams. Although higher education is filled with classroom assignments that require coordination with other students, colleges and universities do not do a very good job developing the skills needed to make teams work successfully. This area of know-how involves learning how to "step up" and exercise leadership.

Developing leadership skills is not about learning how to create a charismatic personality or "be the boss." Instead, *leadership* is about discovering how to keep people moving forward in a way that makes use of the skills and knowledge they individually can offer in service to a common goal. Working in groups and teams requires an understanding of how to influence others, how to resolve conflicts, how to motivate others and how to manage personalities and behaviors in a productive way. This is a tall order for anyone, much less college-age students.

You may have to look for opportunities outside of the classroom to help you develop collaborative and leadership skills. Student government clearly offers one path for practicing and developing your skills at working with others. But there are plenty of opportunities for working with others on campus. Join a club, especially one that appeals to your "fire" or passion, prove yourself as a contributing member and then step into leadership roles. If you pledge a sorority or fraternity, volunteer to organize activities. Get involved in community service projects, in political campaigns or in church mission activities. Or, if none of the extracurricular options available on campus appeal to you, look around at what issue needs addressing and form your own group.

Know How to Share What You Know

Increasingly, an individual's knowledge is only valuable when it is combined with the knowledge of others. This is called joining the "knowledge flow." In the working world, knowledge is flowing all around and through organizations. Being able to bridge knowledge boundaries, or, in other words, being able to reach out to others who aren't focused on the same thing you are and share what you know, is a valuable skill. Developing your ability to communicate in a way that is simple, clear and meaningful will draw others to you and enhance your own knowledge, as well as the knowledge of others.

As strange as it may sound, part of what you can learn from your college experience is how to become an effective teacher. Sharing knowledge is the essence of teaching. Now, your professors aren't likely to turn their classes over to you so that you can practice this valuable skill. Undergraduates rarely get opportunities to serve as teaching assistants. However, if you have the aptitude, you should consider tutoring other students. You'll be helping them while helping yourself gain practice in motivating and training others. Or you could look into whether your college offers a student ambassador program. Student ambassadors share their knowledge of classes, extracurricular activities and even the best burger joints to recruit prospects and help new students adjust to life on campus.

Ways to Get Know-How
Through the College Experience

One thing you can count on at college is that you will experience problems. Problems are universal: problems with your roommate, problems with financial aid, problems with a professor, problems with scheduling. College also is an environment in which many students feel empowered to take on larger problems: advocating for better food in the cafeteria, improving the social climate on campus, calling attention to global warming, preventing domestic abuse, educating others about date rape, saving the seals or treating animals humanely.

When faced with a problem or dilemma, you have two choices: You can deal with the problem, or you can leave it for someone else. Those who want to build their know-how will do the former rather than the latter. The greater your capacity to address problems, the greater your know-how. Think about it: You can't solve a problem without understanding how to create a solution. That requires a combination of knowledge and practice. You also need to develop the communication skills that will enable you to persuade others to buy-in to *your* solution and not someone else's. "Creative problem-solving" is one of those broadly applicable skills that employers crave. But problem-solving, like decision-making, takes practice. The more opportunity you find to take what you're learning in the classroom and apply it out in the world, the better positioned you will be to succeed on the job – and in life.

Know-How for the Job

Very few jobs are just about the know-what of a field. Most require a significant amount of know-how. You might study the concepts of marketing in your business curriculum, but knowing how to close a sale is a skill that requires practice and experience. Although engineers

What Does This Mean for You?

Know How to Learn: Understand the problem.

Whether dealing with the mysteries of financial aid or why people won't recycle, the first step when tackling a problem is to understand the nuts and bolts of the situation. Your effectiveness increases by having more information and making sure that you are on top of the issue. The process of acquiring this information is knowing how to learn.

You can employ your basic library research skills; you can ask questions; you can interview others; you can collect data; you can do any number of things to make sure that you become an "expert" in the issue or problem you are interested in. The skills that are used to discover the way to crack your favorite video game are the same skills you use to crack any problem.

What does this have to do with college? Colleges make it easy to learn about problems. There are experts in almost every field. You probably have a library filled with books and electronic resources. The whole institution is set up to give you access to the information you need. In the real world (the world of work), people who can address problems are valuable. Being able to find good information, integrate it, synthesize it and communicate it to others is fundamental to success in any field. This is a skill that crosses all disciplines and majors. You don't even have to take this on alone. In colleges and universities of any size, there are student organizations and clubs that can get you started in learning about whatever problem you want to tackle. For universities, this is called "student engagement," and it is an important predictor of student success. So the reason to get involved in student organizations on campus is not just to pad your resume, but to practice the process of knowing how to learn, which can be useful throughout your career.

Know How to Work With Others: Harness the power of collaboration.

One of the hardest skills to learn is teamwork. If you are lucky enough to play on a sports team, you might be a few steps ahead, especially if you realize that what makes a team work on the field or the court is the same set of dynamics that makes a team work in class, on campus or in the work world.

Working with others is hard. It can be great, but you almost always will find yourself working with people who make you crazy. Welcome to the rest of your life! College is a great place to try to figure out how to work with others to solve problems or effect change. The downside risk is low, and the upside may study physics, successfully taking concepts from the drawing board – or computer program – to the field is a practiced skill. Plenty of construction workers with far less formal education have a better practical understanding of the "physics of the field" because they have been, well, practicing the skills.

Higher education has begun to embrace the value of know-how by encouraging students, even requiring them in some fields, to engage in internships and co-operative learning programs. Some colleges have long understood the value of enhancing classroom knowledge with on-the-job learning. The University of Cincinnati launched the nation's first co-operative education model back in 1906 and now has more than 5,000 participants, making it the largest such program at a public U.S. institution. Over the past decade or so, an increasing number of colleges have begun to encourage students to do internships and co-op work while in college. The practice has expanded, but students and even professors tend to treat these programs more as opportunities to network and "get a foot in the door" than as valuable extensions of classroom learning and rich environments for building know-how.

If you aren't able to land an internship or a co-op – which, in this economy, has become tougher for young people to do – how else can you move from know-what to know-how? Lucky for you, there are increasingly more opportunities for you to do just that.

While at the university, you will probably hear the phrase "service learning." These out-of-the-classroom, hands-on experiences are growing in popularity on university campuses as ways to appeal to socially conscious young people. Campus Compact, a national coalition of nearly 1,200 colleges and universities, surveys its members annually to determine their support for service activities. For 2008-2009, about a third of all students who attended potential of these life lessons is enormous.

Even if you don't want to take on a major issue on campus, you aren't going to avoid having to work with others. Team assignments are part of the standard bag of tricks for many college professors. The problem is that you and your fellow students are usually left to your own devices in terms of figuring out how to make these assignments work. Knowing how to work with others can be the difference between a group experience that is memorable and one that is pure torture. There is a big difference in working with others and just having a group of people assigned to the same project. If you can figure out how to motivate your fellow students to work together and cooperate, you are developing a valuable skill that will translate into any job environment. Trust us, it's harder than you think. Just look at how little working together goes on in Congress these days.

There are a lot of tools and techniques you can learn to help you develop this skill. Believe it or not, your professors have some pretty good advice about how to make teams run better. The key here is "intentionality." Just having the experience of being on a team isn't magically going to allow you to develop the skill of motivating others. You have to work at it.

Know How to Share What You Know: Practice communicating.

When people talk about the importance of communication skills, they usually are referring to mastering basic writing skills and making sure that you know how to use Word and PowerPoint. Although having basic communication know-how is important, just having those technical skills doesn't make you effective at sharing your ideas with others. You can have the greatest idea in the world, but if you can't make a compelling case to "sell" that idea to others, your billion-dollar innovation isn't going anywhere. Just as using campus problems and class assignments helps you know how to learn and know how to work with others, these challenges also allow you to practice communicating in ways that influence others. That's the kind of communication skill that will set you apart in the marketplace. Communicating in ways that are effective and persuasive is valuable. Think about it, what good is knowing lots about a problem on campus or in the world and attracting other like-minded people to your efforts if you lack the ability to persuade people who are unaware, people who disagree and people with the power to effect change?

If you can put all three skill sets together, you can make big contributions in whatever field you choose to pursue.

member schools participated in community service, service learning and civic engagement activities. More than 60 percent of participating schools had designated academic service-learning courses.

Service activities can be great opportunities to develop know-how related to your area of interest. Service learning comes in two forms: One type might be community service activities (now required on many campuses). The other type might be in the form of some service opportunity related to your academic field. For example, if you are studying elementary education, a service learning experience might be working as a teacher's aide at a local elementary school as part of a class requirement. Seek out faculty who create these types of opportunities.

Enhancing your employability means looking for opportunities to practice what you know and make use of some different mental muscles. A lot of the extracurricular activities that college counselors urge students to pursue are important opportunities for developing know-how. But you won't get the full advantage of these experiences unless you really test yourself when you have the chance. It's easy to put things on your resume, but working to gain the skills that will set you apart is a different sort of test altogether.

Cram Session

- Look for hands-on learning opportunities through internships, co-operative education or community engagement.
- Join a club or other campus organization, show you can be a contributing member and then step up for more challenging roles to practice your leadership skills.
- Practice communicating in ways that are not only clear but also persuasive.

Key Concepts:
gap year
apprenticeship
certification
self-employment

Chapter 12
College Isn't Right for Everyone – Despite What "Everyone" Says

In earlier chapters, we explored which college option might represent the best investment for you based on your academic and financial capital. Yet, that discussion might lead you to believe that some form of the traditional four-year bachelor's degree is the path everyone should take. In August 2010, President Obama explained the urgency behind his goal to raise the nation's college graduation rate to 60 percent within 10 years, saying: "The single most important thing we can do is to make sure we've got a world-class education system for everybody. That is a prerequisite for prosperity." Although we would tend to agree with the President that access to education beyond high school is critical to the nation's overall prosperity, we differ with his implication that a traditional, four-year college degree is the right path for practically everyone.

Truth be told, large numbers of students each year head off to college even though they probably shouldn't be there – at least not right away. Some lack the skills; some lack the time and money; some lack the desire. If you fall into any one of those categories, you should think carefully before you decide to "go with the flow" to college because people – parents, teachers, reporters, politicians, even the President – keep telling you that's what you should do.

Lacking the aptitude, the resources or the desire to go to college can dramatically affect your likelihood of making it to graduation. *As we have said before, if you are going to go to college, you have to finish – you have to get that degree – in order for you to see a return on your college investment. Otherwise, you're largely wasting your time and your money.*

We know that's a shocking statement – especially given the importance of education for your individual prosperity, as well as the nation's long-term competitiveness. Those stories warning of U.S. workers losing ground to better-educated ones in other parts of the world are true. If you as a worker and we as a nation are going to maintain a comfortable standard of living, then advanced education and skill development will be central to that goal. But notice that we have repeatedly said *education*. College is one path to the education you'll need to compete in the 21st century global marketplace, but *it isn't the only one*. For many students, college (right now) is the wrong path. The obvious evidence of that is how many students go but don't graduate.

If you are one of those students who questions whether college is the right path for you, first give yourself credit for sizing up your own circumstances and resisting the "everybody's doing it" logic. However, you should assume that to get the life you want, some sort of additional education or hands-on training will be necessary. Here are some alternative strategies that might make sense for someone who wants to consider something other than the traditional college path after high school.

Alternative Strategy 1: Take a "gap" year. Since the time you were 5, maybe even 2, you've been in school. It's understandable that you're ready for a break from the grind. Maybe you don't know what you want to be doing in five years or even what you are interested in right now. You are not alone. Most kids your age don't. Maybe you recognize that there's a big world out there, and you want to see some of it before you get held in place by the commitments of school, work, marriage, kids and mortgage. Plenty of legitimate learning goes on outside of classrooms. We also have to admit that all the heavy expectations now put on young people sure do seem to wring the fun out of learning.

Increasingly, burnt-out students are choosing to explore the world outside of the classroom before they head off to college. The practice of taking a break between high school and college for self-discovery is more common in Europe, but a "gap year" is gaining acceptance in the United States.

Some colleges, particularly elite private ones, are openly supportive. Princeton University, for example, launched a pilot Bridge Year Program in fall 2009, allowing students accepted to the college to spend a year after high school engaged in international public service. A gap year may be just what you need to restore your love of school, but you should talk to your college of choice about your plan before you take your break. Remember, this isn't meant to prolong the college-choice process and encourage procrastination; it's supposed to give you time for reflection and discovery, which, in theory, will help you be a more focused, determined student after you arrive on campus.

What would be a productive gap year experience? Focus on opportunities for personal growth. You could volunteer for AmeriCorps or the affiliated City Year, actually earning a living allowance, as well as money for college, while you tutor schoolchildren, build houses or otherwise engage in community service.

As long as you aren't expecting your parents to pay for it, you could travel abroad to get a better understanding of the world while you try to find your place in it. While you're exploring the globe, you're also developing valuable skills, such as problem-solving and time-management, as well as gaining important insights about yourself and the rest of the world.

Before you venture down this gap year path, however, you should recognize that postponing college, whether for one year or 10, comes with significant consequences and risks. It may be costly. You'll be behind your peers. It may take you longer to get started in your career. Plus, as you get older, life tends to get more complicated, making it harder to go back to school. Not impossible, but definitely harder. Older students who didn't have the opportunity to go on to college or who failed to finish what they started are returning to school in ever greater numbers. Many succeed, but even they would be quick to admit the difficulty of balancing school with the demands of work, marriage, kids and mortgages. But you're young. You're probably not worried about such things just yet.

Alternative Strategy 2: Work for yourself. Maybe you already have an idea of what you want to do. Maybe your goal is not to work for somebody else. Instead, you want to be your own boss. More than 99 percent of all U.S. employers are small businesses, according to the Small Business Administration, and those small businesses employ about half of the entire private-sector workforce.

Going into business for yourself is a risky move – only about 30 percent of all new business start-ups survive for 10 years, according to Census Bureau data – but it can be both financially and personally rewarding. If you have a pot of money, a business idea that serves a real market, the risk-taking mindset of an entrepreneur and the drive to work 60 or 80 hours a week, then starting your own business might be a great idea. In your case, perhaps the money you would have spent pursuing a bachelor's degree could be put to better use building your business.

Making the calculated choice to invest in a business plan instead of a bachelor's degree doesn't mean that you should forget about college entirely. You may find it helpful to take a few classes in management, finance and business strategy. You may not need four years of coursework, but you will need to develop the critical skills and knowledge base to run a business profitably.

Alternative Strategy 3: Become the apprentice. A generation ago, most workers went directly into the workforce after they graduated high school. They learned the skills they needed on the job. Your grandparents probably followed this path, and maybe even your parents. It was a path that worked for many middle-income families, and it still could work for you.

Centuries ago, most crafts and trades were learned through apprenticeship. Whether you wanted to be a printer or a blacksmith, you would likely spend a number of years working with a tradesman to learn the necessary skills. Today, electrical, plumbing, carpentry and other trades tend to be the most familiar apprenticeship programs, but there are opportunities to learn many skills using the same method.

By the Numbers

The Occupational Outlook Handbook predicts 13 percent growth through 2018 in the need for carpenters. In 2006, there were nearly 1.5 million people working as carpenters; the OOH expects there to be nearly 1.7 million workers employed as carpenters by 2018. The median hourly wage for carpenters in 2008 was $18.72, or nearly $39,000 per year. Top earners made nearly $70,000. Residential building construction employs the most contractors and pays above-average wages.

In general, the OOH predicts job prospects in the skilled trades to be very good in the coming years because, in addition to increase in demand, a large number of experienced workers are approaching retirement age. Median pay for a plumber or pipefitter was nearly $22 an hour, or about $46,000 annually. The average annual median salary for electricians was nearly $50,000 in 2008. Top earners in both fields pulled in nearly $80,000.

Anatomy of Apprenticeship

Local trade unions and chapters of national associations often jointly sponsor apprenticeship programs. Electrician programs, for example, consist of 144 hours of classroom instruction and 2,000 hours of on-the-job training for each of the four years of education. In the classroom, apprentices learn about electrical theory and codes, blueprints and safety practices. Experienced electricians supervise apprentices in progressively more challenging tasks, from drilling holes and fabricating conduit to connecting wiring and designing electrical systems. Although having a high school diploma or GED is the only academic requirement for acceptance into apprenticeship programs, work in the plumbing, carpentry or electrical trades requires an understanding and mastery of basic math, algebra, geometry and some trigonometry.

Plumbing apprenticeship programs tend to last five years, each consisting of at least 216 hours in the classroom and up to 2,000 hours on the job. These are challenging programs, with apprentices working the same number of hours as the more experienced, or journeyman, workers and going to school at night. Pay tends to be a percentage of the wages of experienced workers. Apprentices accepted into the United Association of Journeymen plumbing and pipefitting union program are paid at a rate equal to about half the earnings of journeymen plumbers.

Classes offered through vocational schools and training academies sometimes help students gain entrance into apprenticeship programs and entry-level pay advantage. After completing an apprentice program, workers in the trades often are required to take state examinations that test their knowledge and skills in order to be licensed. Workers in the trades also may continue their education by taking periodic safety classes, training on new equipment and procedures, and learning management skills to become a supervisor or a private contractor. Supervisors and private contractors need to be able to understand bid specifications and estimate the costs and time involved in completing projects. Workers in the trades increasingly are pursuing certification in particular areas of competence and expertise.

In the best circumstances, apprenticeship creates an engaging learning environment by combining classroom instruction, hands-on training and long-term mentoring. We say long-term because many apprenticeship programs may last four or five years, not that much different than the time it would take you to complete a bachelor's degree. Yet, unlike college, those accepted into apprenticeship get paid as they learn.

The U.S. Department of Labor has a Registered Apprenticeship program that provides information on training for hundreds of career fields. (Visit the DOL's Office of Apprenticeship website at www.doleta.gov/oa/) The website provides a link to information about opportunities in each state. There are 28,000 programs nationwide, which include partnerships with businesses, labor unions, trade associations, and two- and four-year colleges.

Although many of the apprenticeship opportunities support the construction and manufacturing industries, more than 700 new programs serving in-demand fields such as geospatial technology, nanotechnology, emergency preparedness and renewable energy were added in 2007. Apprentice programs have been developed to address the growing need for workers in various aspects of the health-care industry, such as medical transcriptionist, surgical technologist, prosthetic technician and biomedical equipment technician. Additional programs are being developed and piloted.

Of the roughly 3 million students who completed high school in 2007, about 2 million enrolled in either a four-year or two-year college, according to the National Center for Education Statistics. By comparison, 212,000 men and women entered the Registered Apprenticeship system in the same year. That number included young people fresh out of high school, as well as older adults looking for opportunities to improve their career options. That same year, 35,300 graduated from the apprenticeship program with certifications recognized nationwide.

Hundreds of two-year and four-year colleges have partnered with the Registered Apprenticeship system to offer bachelor's and associate's degrees along with apprenticeship certificates. Businesses and industries, as apprenticeship sponsors, pay the bulk of training costs, with the construction industry alone contributing an estimated $250 million yearly. According to the Department of Labor, the average yearly salary of those completing Registered Apprenticeship programs in 2007 was more than $50,000.

Alternative Strategy 4: Get certified. If four years of instruction, even combined with hands-on learning, seem longer than you would like to commit, consider one of the many short-term certification programs that are available.

If you spent your high school years gaming and thrive in the realm of technology and gadgetry, you may want to consider the field of computer tech support. A one-year certificate program in information technology might help you get there. Salaries vary widely, and many jobs may require a four-year degree, but the Occupational Outlook Handbook notes that employers are becoming more flexible about accepting an associate's degree or even relevant experience. Help-desk workers may earn less than $30,000 annually to start, according to Robert Half Technology, but starting salaries for desktop support analysts approach $50,000 or more.

A wealth of training, testing and certification programs is available in a broad range of fields through community colleges, business and vocational schools, and non-profit trade organizations. For example, the International Association of Administrative Professionals offers a three-part exam, covering office technology, administration and management, to achieve the designation of Certified Professional Secretary and also offers more advanced testing as a Certified Administrative Professional. The IAAP suggests that certification boosts earnings by about 7 percent.

The International Virtual Assistants Association has three certifications available: Certified Virtual Assistant,

Ethics Checked Virtual Assistant and Real Estate Virtual Assistant. Workers new to the field or those more experienced can pay a $120 fee to have their skills tested in areas such as word processing, data management, bookkeeping, writing and editing, and web design. The Occupational Outlook Handbook predicts that the need for executive secretaries and administrative assistants will grow by 13 percent through 2018, with a median salary expectation of more than $40,000.

If you have a mechanical knack, combined with an understanding of computers and electronics, you may find that one of the roughly 170 Aviation Maintenance Technician schools certified by the Federal Aviation Administration (FAA) provides you with quick access to a job that suits yours interests. Completing the required coursework and training takes one to two years, but aviation mechanics can expect to earn nearly $25 per hour. Median pay for 2008 was more than $51,000.

Training to become a licensed practical nurse (LPN) may offer you a short path to the workforce while keeping your options open for improving your pay through increased training. The Occupational Outlook Handbook expects good job opportunities for licensed practical and vocational nurses through 2016. Programs, which consist of both classroom and clinical training, may cost as little as $3,000 for tuition in some states. Passing a licensure test after completing the program is required to become a practicing nurse. Median annual pay for LPNs was $39,000 in 2008, according to the Bureau of Labor Statistics, with salaries starting at around $30,000.

Licensed practical nurses may find they want to continue their education to become registered nurses (RNs) through a two-year associate's degree program or a four-year bachelor's of science in nursing program. Many health-care employers may offer tuition reimbursement for the increased training. This is a cost-effective plan for accessing valuable education. RNs earned an annual median salary of $62,450 in 2008.

If you can't imagine being a nurse, there are many other jobs in the growing health-care industry that require only short-term, sometimes on-the-job training. Electrocardiography (EKG) technicians are usually trained on the job over a span of four to six weeks, according to the Occupational Outlook Handbook. Previous experience in the health-care field, perhaps as an aide or an orderly, tends to make you a better candidate for EKG technician training. More advanced skills may be obtained through longer on-the-job training or through certificate programs. Median pay for cardiovascular technicians and technologists was more than $47,000 in 2008.

The growth in the health-care industry is even spurring growth in certain areas of manufacturing. Biomedical equipment technicians, also known as medical equipment repairers, are skilled in working on the electronic, electromechanical and hydraulic equipment used in hospitals and other medical environments, such as defibrillators, heart monitors, X-ray machines, voice-controlled operating tables and electric wheelchairs. Employment in this area is expected to grow by 27 percent through 2018, with workers earning more than $41,000 on average. Despite the growing high-tech nature of the job, many medical equipment repairers continue to learn their skills either on the job or through short educational programs. With more complicated equipment, workers may need to pursue additional education and take a test to become certified. The rapid change in this industry means you should expect to constantly be refreshing your skills to remain up-to-date on new technologies and devices.

Alternative Strategy 5: Get personal. In an economy that has seen customer-service jobs outsourced to India and manufacturing work sent to China, occupations requiring face-to-face interaction with customers, such as hairstylists, massage therapists, manicurists, skin care specialists and fitness trainers, are expected to see good growth in the coming years. In obese America, the number of fitness trainers is expected to grow by 27 percent to roughly 298,000 workers by 2016. Median annual salary for 2008 was $29,210, although top earners received $60,670.

Group fitness instructors may begin their learning by taking classes. Special certification programs are available to teach classes such as Pilates and yoga. Personal trainers may have earned bachelor's degrees in exercise science, physical education or kinesiology, and certification is increasingly required.

Hairstylists, cosmetologists, and skin care specialists are expected to see faster than average growth and good job prospects but keen competition for jobs at higher-paying salons, according to the Occupational Outlook Handbook. State-licensed training programs, which are offered through postsecondary schools as well as high schools, typically last a few months. Personal appearance workers, of which there are expected to be more than 940,000 by 2016, are required to be licensed.

Entry-level wages for personal appearance workers are often below $10 an hour. However, in-demand experienced workers, especially those in higher-paying salons with a regular customer base, may earn significantly higher wages. In 2008, the median annual earnings for hairstylists was $23,140. The bottom 10 percent of earners made just $15,530, and the top 10 percent made $42,460, on average.

Many of these personal service jobs are lower paying, and many workers in these areas tend to be self-employed. One way to improve your earnings potential is to open your own salon. But being a successful salon owner requires a different set of skills than simply being a good hairstylist. Working in a salon while you learn what you can from the owner is a good way to start acquiring those necessary skills. Taking a few business courses to help with your management and bookkeeping skills would be another good idea to help you along your way to small business ownership.

Fitness trainers, hairstylists and workers in other service-sector jobs benefit from an outgoing personality that helps attract new clients and interpersonal skills that help them maintain a loyal customer base. Such skills also come in handy in the sales profession. Sales jobs often have no formal education requirements although a college degree may be important for moving up into management positions.

Retail sales positions tend to be rather low-paying, with department store and specialty store workers typically earning less than $10 an hour. However, wholesale and manufacturing sales representatives tend to earn much more. Median salaries are roughly $50,000, with sales representatives in technical and scientific fields earning $70,000 or more, on average. The top 10 percent of sales earners made more than $120,000 in 2006. Nearly half of all wholesale and manufacturing sales representatives have no college degree, but 38 percent have a bachelor's degree. And employers are increasingly looking for a college degree for entry-level sales jobs in these areas. Inexpensive continuing education classes that focus on public speaking, etiquette and personal appearance may also be a good investment in the sales field.

Alternative Strategy 6: Spend a few years with Uncle Sam. Joining the military has long been an alternative to college. The military offers the benefits of leaving home and seeking adventure just like a "gap year." All that with three square meals a day, housing and a paycheck. Plus, there's the added motivation of serving your country.

All of the branches of the military offer entry straight

out of high school. Generally, recruiters are looking for a few good men and women who have a good attitude. Although your academic scores might give you more options in your military training placement, just having the high school diploma should be enough for an entry-level position in the military chain of command. The military is a good place to learn both personal discipline and marketable skills. In addition, after you have completed your military commitment, the government often will help pay for your education.

One young man we know, Jay, went into the Marines straight out of high school. He served in both Iraq wars and became certified in the military medical corps. After completing a few hitches in the Marines, Jay went into the Reserves and enrolled at a regional public university. His university counted several of his military courses as academic credit, and he was able to complete a business degree in only three years. Because of the discipline and attitude he developed in the Marines, he had a great work ethic and a "can-do" confidence that left some of his younger classmates in the dust. After graduation, Jay was hired by a Fortune 500 company that was impressed with both his military experience and his college degree. Jay is currently earning a six-figure salary.

Another young man leveraged a commitment to the National Guard into a college degree. Clay entered the National Guard in his early 20s and used financial support from the Guard to pay for a bachelor's degree while also working full time and supporting a family. Clay went up in the ranks, and, after twice being called into service (once after 9/11 and again for Afghanistan), he will retire from military service with a 20-year pension and the rank of colonel.

Whether as a career choice or as a way to transition from high school to a different career path, the military can be a good option for young people who are not currently interested in college. Many young men and women make the military their lifelong career. Others take the training they gain through military service and leverage it into a job in the same area, but as a civilian. There is nothing in civilian life that will teach teamwork and self-discipline like the military. This is why many employers actively seek people with military experience. Military service isn't easy, and it isn't for everyone, but if you want a rewarding challenge, it might be for you.

Alternative Strategy 7: Recognize when you already possess in-demand skills. Some people do have natural gifts. If you are lucky enough to be one of them, you may be better off bypassing the traditional college path and sharing your talents with the world. We put this strategy last because few 18-year-olds are so talented that they can pursue their fields of interest without some form of post-high-school training. But there are those whose considerable talents are already of value in the marketplace. We know a young man who had a natural curiosity about computers and an affinity for programming. He had been writing his own programs in his spare time at home and had taken every high school computer programming class available. He even started a club for his fellow students.

His high school required seniors to spend two weeks shadowing workers on the job. This young man, we'll call him "Alex," was fortunate enough to get a local mid-sized software development firm to allow him to come in for the two-week project. The company saw a rare spark in this teenager and took the unusual step of offering him an internship for the summer. His supervisors gave him small projects but observed his eagerness and, most importantly, his largely self-taught skill. At the end of the summer, the boss of the firm toyed with offering Alex a permanent, full-time job – paying $50,000 to start. The boss considered the price a steal for a raw but natural talent.

In the end, the boss never offered the job. He didn't want to derail Alex and his parents' college plans. Alex had been accepted at his school of choice – a name-brand private college with a respectable but not spectacular ranking. Alex's parents are both college-educated, first-generation immigrants with expectations that their eldest child would find even greater success through education. The boss, too, is college-educated, the fourth generation in his family to earn a college degree, and he expects his own children will make it five. It would be an understatement to say that Alex's parents and the boss are biased toward higher education.

Yet, is college really the right choice for Alex? In terms of providing a competitive economic advantage and a rewarding return on investment, it's hard to make the case. Certainly, there are many benefits of college that aren't measured simply in dollars and cents. The opportunity for self-discovery and personal growth can be immeasurable and life-changing. But a college degree today, with the considerable sacrifice and investment required to obtain it, is touted more for the economic advantage it affords than for the intellectual development.

If Alex had been offered and taken the computer programming job right out of high school, he presumably would have earned at least $200,000 in those four years that he otherwise would have spent in college classrooms learning the theory behind what he was actually doing on the job. But instead of enjoying the benefits of a good-paying job, Alex and his parents will pay a hefty investment in a college degree. Those four years of college will cost Alex and his family roughly $100,000 in direct outlay and put him nearly $20,000 in debt. In this somewhat extraordinary case, there's also the $200,000 in lost wages that Alex *could* have been earning for those four years, which potentially brings the total cost to him for his four years of college to an eye-popping $320,000.

The economic rationale behind investing in a college degree is that it will lead to rewards in the marketplace that, over time, far exceed the cost of that education. Perhaps Alex's best bet would have been to find the best college near his software job and enroll part time while working full time. Perhaps he even could have negotiated for part-time work while going to school full time. That would have limited the loss of his potential earnings while still providing the opportunity to have a flavor of the college experience. It also would have given him a valuable combination of classroom and on-the-job skills.

College isn't the only path to career success, but realistically, if you want to be able to take care of yourself and any future family, you will need some sort of education beyond high school. We've given you just a few ideas. Now that you know what to look for, you might even bring up some of these alternative strategies the next time you have one of those talks with your parents about "the future." Even they may not realize the range of options that are out there for someone who just isn't ready for or interested in another four years of traditional schooling.

Cram Session

- Every year large numbers of students head off to college even though they probably shouldn't be there – at least not right away. Some lack the skills; some lack the time and money; some lack the desire. If you fall into any one of those categories, you should think carefully before you decide to "go with the flow."
- If you decide that heading off to college isn't the right path for you, you should understand that some sort of education beyond high school is likely going to be necessary for you to succeed in today's job market.
- Starting a business, becoming an apprentice, getting certified or joining the military offer alternative career paths.

Key Concepts:
lifelong learning
graduate and professional degrees
refreshing skills

Chapter 13
Staying in the Game
With Lifelong Learning

If you're looking at college as something you do for four years (or more) right after high school to check off your "to do" list, you probably need to think again. That's not an assumption you should make in an economic environment that runs on knowledge. As the technological era shows, knowledge changes quickly. What's cutting-edge today is quaint a decade or even a year from now. Good jobs today won't be the same 30 years from now. That's how *your* work future differs so dramatically from your grandparents' and even your parents'.

In the 21st century, you can't count on jobs and skills staying the same. That means you need to plan on actively acquiring new skills and new knowledge throughout your career. If you are to succeed in this rapidly changing, global job market, you have to be committed to *lifelong learning*. That means if new technology or new procedures come along that affect your job, you need to embrace those changes and adapt to the new working environment by always being willing to learn new things. It may not matter whether you learn these innovations in the classroom, on the job or by teaching them to yourself. What definitely matters is that you learn them.

Some professions require that you constantly update

your skills and learn new techniques or protocols. People who work in fields such as nursing, teaching, social work and pharmacy are required to complete a specified number of continuing education credits within a certain number of years. In the many fields that don't require workers to continue their learning and training, those who experience a job interruption often find that their stagnant skills no longer match what is being demanded and rewarded in the marketplace.

If you don't believe us, try asking the hundreds of thousands of manufacturing workers who have lost their jobs over the past decade. Whether in Ohio, North Carolina or any other state, there are horror stories of middle-age workers who had the same job for decades only to see it completely disappear due to technology changes, outsourcing or recession. Lacking skills demanded in today's marketplace, many of these workers have had to take lower-paying jobs.

Others have taken advantage of retraining programs or have returned to school to learn a completely new profession. Think about how difficult it must be for a man who has spent his life as a tool-and-die maker to return to the classroom after 20 years to study to be a nurse. Or how difficult it is for a woman who worked in a textile mill to retrain as a computer technician.

You can insulate yourself from some of that difficulty if you commit now to refreshing your skill set and broadening your knowledge base throughout your work life. We're not saying that a commitment to lifelong learning will protect you from job loss or other disruptions. What it will do is improve the odds that you will be able to bounce back from whatever market upheaval occurs.

Long-term Strategy 1: Go immediately for a graduate degree. Some of you may start on your lifelong learning path before the ink on your bachelor's degree is even dry. Remember, workers holding graduate degrees earn, on average, more money than workers who don't. The U.S. Census Bureau demonstrated that reality in the 2002 study called "The Big Payoff: Educational Attainment and Synthetic Estimates of Work-Life Earnings." Sure, the title isn't nearly as exciting as if the government had called it "Stay in School and Make More Money," but that's the gist of the report: Higher educational levels, on average, pay off in higher earnings.

Workers who had master's degrees and worked year-round earned, on average, $62,300 annually, or about $10,000 more than full-time workers who only had earned a bachelor's degree. According to the Census report, workers with master's degrees had salaries that more than doubled the full-time earnings of workers who had only a high school diploma. Workers who had completed a doctorate earned, on average, $89,400 per year – or 43 percent more than master's degree holders – and those who had attained a professional degree earned $109,600 – or 76 percent more than workers with master's degrees.

Over a lifetime, those differences in pay add up big time. In addition to higher wages, advanced degrees tend to bring job security. Better-educated workers are less likely to be unemployed than workers without degrees. According to the Bureau of Labor Statistics, only 4.9 percent of workers with a bachelor's degree or higher were unemployed in September 2009; that compares to 10.8 percent of workers with only a high school diploma.

Back in Chapter 1, we talked about how the market value of a bachelor's degree is likely to decline as more and more young people head off to and graduate from college. Pursuing even more education is one way to set yourself apart from the large number of job applicants with bachelor's degrees. However, a graduate degree will cost you more in time and money, it may require you to take on a higher level of debt, and it will delay your entry into the workforce. If you plan

In-Demand Occupations

The Occupational Outlook Handbook lists which jobs requiring advanced educational degrees are expected to see the largest percentage increase through 2016. They are:

The occupations requiring advanced degrees that the OOH predicts will see the largest growth in numbers through 2016 are:

MASTER'S DEGREE

Mental health counselors
Mental and substance abuse social workers
Marriage and family counselors
Physical therapists
Physician assistants

MASTER'S DEGREE

Clergy
Physical therapists
Mental health and substance abuse social workers
Educational, vocational and school counselors
Rehabilitation counselors

DOCTORAL DEGREE

Postsecondary teachers
Computer and information research scientists
Medical scientists (except epidemiologists)
Biochemists and biophysicists
Clinical, counseling and school psychologists

DOCTORAL DEGREE

Postsecondary teachers
Clinical, counseling and school psychologists
Medical scientists (except epidemiologists)
Computer and information research scientists
Biochemists and biophysicists

PROFESSIONAL DEGREE

Veterinarians
Pharmacists
Chiropractors
Physicians and surgeons
Optometrists

PROFESSIONAL DEGREE

Physicians and surgeons
Lawyers
Pharmacists
Veterinarians
Dentists

to pursue a master's degree or doctorate, you may want to return to our discussion of the College Payback Ratio in Chapter 3 to calculate what you can expect from your added investment.

Long-term Strategy 2: Explore options for continuing your studies part time while you work. If you can't afford or can't stomach the idea of an extra year or more to earn that master's or professional degree, there are plenty of options for taking your education beyond the bachelor's level. More and more colleges are making it easier for students to return to school after being in the workforce for a while to complete a graduate or professional degree part time. Evening, Saturday and online classes are increasingly common. Some schools even offer shorter, more intensive sessions to help you complete the degree more quickly.

Yes, being a part-time student means the coursework will likely take you longer to complete. That one-year master's program may take you three or four years if you can only manage one class per semester. Waiting until you're already in the workforce to pursue a graduate degree does have some advantages, though. For one thing, you'll be earning money so you likely will be able to pay your way instead of taking on debt. For another thing, work experience will help shape what you want out of an advanced degree. You'll have a better understanding of what you like, what you're good at and what is rewarded in the marketplace. This is valuable insight to have. Finally, some employers still have tuition subsidies and may help pay for your graduate work.

Long-term Strategy 3: Get certified. Perhaps you have no interest in a rigid graduate program. Perhaps you decided that a bachelor's degree wasn't even right for you. There are still plenty of opportunities for you to pursue additional learning that will potentially pay off in the marketplace. Certificate programs are ways to acquire specific skills. These programs tend to be short-term – perhaps a few months, maybe only a few days. Unlike more structured academic degree programs, certificate programs tend to be more closely aligned with the business environment. They are created as a way of quickly responding to workforce needs and tend to develop out of a demand for specific skills. Some certificate programs don't require a bachelor's degree, but other certificates are specifically created to help people with a bachelor's degree update their knowledge and skills without having to spend the time and money needed to complete a master's degree.

For example, GIS – geographic information systems – is a technological advancement in mapping and analyzing problems. It is a computer-enhanced tool that has changed the surveying and cartography industry. People in that field who have updated their skills to incorporate this tool can expect better job prospects than those who haven't. The Occupational Outlook Handbook expects employment in the field of surveying, cartography and photogrammetry (a 3-D technique for measuring coordinates using photographs) to grow by nearly 20 percent through 2018. However, those with GIS skills are expected to be in even greater demand. GIS certification programs are available for those with or without a bachelor's degree.

The website www.certificationguide.com indexes nearly 2,900 national certification programs, grouped by occupation. The Society of Manufacturing Engineers offers several programs, including a new Green Manufacturing Specialist Certificate it launched in 2010 with Purdue University's Technical Assistance Program. The International Webmasters Association offers certification for security specialists. The Institute of Hazardous Materials Management claims to have certified more than 15,000 workers in areas such as homeland security, transportation and health sciences. The American Society for Clinical Pathology certifies laboratory technicians.

There are certifications in more areas than you can probably imagine: dog trainer, yoga instructor, horsemanship instructor, sport psychologist and wetland scientist, to name a few. The trick is figuring out which certification programs actually are worth your time and investment. You should do some research before you fork over any money. Will the extra training benefit you in the job market? Will it lead to more pay? Will it improve your odds of moving up or surviving job cuts? Some certificate programs definitely give you a greater return in the marketplace than others. Do some research to figure out which ones.

Long-term Strategy 4: Get hooked on learning – for financial gain and for fun. Throughout this book, we have tried to hammer home the importance of thinking economically about college costs, debt loads and job prospects. As bachelor's degrees become more and more common, these become even more important concerns. However, we would never want to leave you with the notion that education is only about economics. There is much more benefit to learning than simply how much of a financial payoff it is likely to bring you. If you look at learning as a lifelong pursuit – if you think of learning as fluid and self-directed instead of a formal, structured process – then you will begin to see the rewarding possibilities of education.

You may ultimately become a banker by day but choose to take writing classes at night to release your inner creativity. You may become a computer programmer who takes psychology classes to better understand your colleagues. You may become a doctor with a fascination for history. You may become a music teacher who has a passion for learning more about the environment. There are so many opportunities available today that allow you to feed your soul, whether or not that passion will feed your family. You may never use this knowledge in your job, but the experience will reward you in other ways.

Our mother, at the advanced age of 75, decided she wanted to try her hand at carpentry and construction. She enrolled in a class at the local community college. She was the only woman in the class – and the only student over the age of 50. She even had about 20 years on the instructor. Aside from getting an exemption from climbing a ladder to learn roofing skills, she completed every other assignment and delighted in her "A" grade at the end of the term. Now, that class was never going to benefit her economically – unless you count the money she saved by making wooden puzzles to give to all the grandkids as presents. But she got a lot of pleasure from learning new skills and challenging herself.

That wasn't the first time she had gone back to school. Like many teachers of her era, she pursued her master's degree part time while working full time. She took various classes over the years that enhanced her teaching and administrative skills. And she periodically took painting and drawing classes at the local community college. Those classes gave her a creative outlet away from the demands of work and home and primarily were chosen for her own personal growth and enjoyment. However, she was also able to draw on what she learned to offer her own elementary-age students some art awareness during their daily classroom instruction.

You are at the beginning of your journey of lifelong learning. Don't let the idea discourage you. Keep in mind that there are many paths to growth and development. Some of those paths lead to college; others don't. You will be learning in a variety of ways and from a variety of people all of your life. Strive to grasp all that you can and create your own unique path to your future.

Cram Session

- Don't expect your educational needs to end after you complete your bachelor's degree.
- In a rapidly changing global job market, you need to commit to refreshing your skills so that you can keep up.
- Lifelong learning can be fun.

Chapter 14
On Your Own: Worksheets for Sizing Up Your Choices

Worksheet 1: Calculating Your Out-of-Pocket Education Investment

Name of Institution		Example	College A	College B	College C
A. Total Stated Price					
	1. Tuition & Fees	$27,293			
	2. Room & Board	$9,700			
	3. Books & Supplies	$2,500			
B. Rebates					
	1. Scholarships & Grants	$14,973			
	2. Tax Deduction	$1,000			
C. Education Investment (Out of Pocket) Per Year (A minus B)		$23,520			
D. 4-Year Education Investment (Line C x 4)		$94,080			
E. 5-Year Education Investment (Line C x 5)		$117,600			
F. 6-Year Education Investment (Line C x 6)		$141,120			

Worksheet 2: Calculating the Marginal Market Value of Your Future Degree

A. Annual Market Value of an Entry-Level Job in Your Future Field (Median)

B. Annual Market Value of a Job Requiring Only a High School Diploma (Median) $30,000

C. Marginal Market Value of Job (Per Year) (A minus B)

Worksheet 3: Calculating Your College Payback Ratio

Name of Institution	Example	College A	College B	College C
A. 4-Year Education Investment (Worksheet 1, Line D)	$94,080			
B. 5-Year Education Investment (Worksheet 1, Line E)	$117,600			
C. 6-Year Education Investment (Worksheet 1, Line F)	$141,120			
D. Marginal Market Value of Job (Worksheet 2, Line C)	$17,000			

Payback Time in Number of Years After Graduation

	Example	College A	College B	College C
E. College Payback Ratio, 4 Years to Degree (A divided by D)	5.53			
F. College Payback Ratio, 5 Years to Degree (B divided by D)	6.92			
G. College Payback Ratio, 6 Years to Degree (C divided by D)	8.30			

Worksheet 4: Decision Matrix (Unweighted)

Name of School	SELECTIVITY — Do you have the Academic Capital?		STICKER PRICE — Do you have the Financial Capital?		SIZE — How big is your campus comfort zone?		SUCCESS RATE — Does the school get people through?		SCORE
	Average of the 25th and 75th percentiles	Rank based on how close to your score (A)	Net sticker price based on family income	Rank based on net sticker price (B)	Student enrollment	Rank based on student enrollment (C)	6-year graduation rate	Rank based on 6-year graduation rate (D)	Unweighted score (A+B+C+D)
Example	1015	3	$16,354	2	1,882	2	61%	1	8

(A) If you rank seven schools, the school with the ACT or SAT score closest to yours should be ranked No. 1 and the one furthest from your score should be ranked No. 7. Return to Chapter 10 for detailed explanations.

(B) The school with the lowest sticker price should be ranked No. 1. The school with the highest sticker price should be ranked No. 7.

(C) If you prefer LARGE schools, the school with the largest enrollment should be ranked No. 1 and the smallest ranked No. 7. If you prefer SMALL schools, then the school with the smallest enrollment should be ranked No. 1, and the school with the largest should be ranked No. 7.

(D) The school with the highest graduation rate should be ranked No. 1. The school with the lowest graduation rate should be ranked No. 7.

Worksheet 5: Weighted Decision Matrix

Name of the School	Do you have the Academic Capital? SELECTIVITY			Do you have the Financial Capital? STICKER PRICE			How big is your campus comfort zone? SIZE			Does the school get people through? SUCCESS RATE			SCORE
	Average of the 25th and 75th percentile score	Rank based on how close to your score	(A) Weight: How important to you? ___ points*	Net sticker price based on family income	Rank based on net sticker price	(B) Weight: How important to you? ___ points*	Student enrollment	Rank based on student enrollment	(C) Weight: How important to you? ___ points*	6-year graduation rate	Rank based on 6-year graduation rate	(D) Weight: How important to you? ___ points*	Weighted score (A+B+C+D)
Example	1230	3	60	$17,665	2	80	1,216	2	20	81%	1	30	190

*Only you know how important each category is to you. Try dividing 100 points among the four categories. If you're really focused on cost, you might give that category 40 points. If you don't care about size, you might give that category only 10 points. You might give success rate 30 and selectivity 20. Then multiply the weight you gave each category by the rank for each of the four schools.

Online Resources

ACT: www.act.org

Bureau of Labor Statistics' Education Pays:
    www.bls.gov/emp/ep_chart_001.htm

Bureau of Labor Statistics' Occupational Employment Statistics:
    www.bls.gov/oes/

Bureau of Labor Statistics' Occupational Outlook Handbook:
    www.bls.gov/oco

Campus Contact: www.compact.org/

College Board: www.collegeboard.org

College Navigator: http://nces.ed.gov/collegenavigator

Colleges That Change Lives: www.ctcl.org

Education Trust's College Results: www.collegeresults.org

Federal Student Aid: www.studentaid.ed.gov

Free Application for Federal Student Aid: http://www.fafsa.ed.gov

HEATH Resource Center for students with disabilities:
    www.heath.gwu.edu/

Know How 2 Go: www.knowhow2go.org

Making College Pay: www.makingcollegepay.com

National College Access Network: www.collegeaccess.org

National Consumer Law Center, Student Loan Borrower
    Assistance: www.nclc.org/special-projects/student-loan-
    borrower-assistance.html

Project on Student   Debt: http://projectonstudentdebt.org/

Project on Student Debt's Income-Based Repayment:
    www.ibrinfo.org

Security on Campus: www.securityoncampus.org

Student Gateway to the U.S. Government: www.students.gov

U.S. Department of Education's Campus Safety and Security Data
    Analysis Cutting Tool: http://www.ope.ed.gov/security/

U.S. Department of Education's National Center for Education
    Statistics: http://nces.ed.gov/

U.S. Department of Labor's Office of Apprenticeship:
    www.doleta.gov/oa/

Selected References

Arum, R., & Roksa, J. (2011). "Academically Adrift: Limited Learning on College Campuses." University of Chicago Press.

Barton, P. (2002, September). "The Closing of the Education Frontier?" Educational Testing Service. Available: http://www.ets.org/Media/Research/pdf/PICFRONTIER.pdf

Baum, S., Ma, J., & Payea, K. "Education Pays 2010: The Benefits of Higher Education for Individuals and Society." Trends in Higher Education Series. College Board Advocacy & Policy Center. Available: http://trends.collegeboard.org/downloads/Education_Pays_2010.pdf

Baum, S., & Steele, P. (2010). "Who Borrows Most? Bachelor's Degree Recipients with High Levels of Student Debt." Trends in Higher Education Series. College Board Advocacy & Policy Center. Available: http://advocacy.collegeboard.org/sites/default/files/Trends-Who-Borrows-Most-Brief.pdf

"Best College Rankings." U.S. News & World Report. Available: http://colleges.usnews.rankingsandreviews.com/best-colleges.

College Navigator. National Center for Education Statistics. Available: http://nces.ed.gov/collegenavigator/.

Dale, S., & Krueger, A. (Feb. 16, 2011). "Estimating the Return to College Selectivity Over the Career Using Administrative Earning Data." Working Paper No. 563, Princeton University. Available: http://www.irs.princeton.edu/pubs/pdfs/563.pdf

Day, J., & Newburger, E. (2002, July). "The Big Payoff: Educational Attainment and Synthetic Estimates of Work-Life Earnings." U.S. Census Bureau, Current Population Reports. Available: http://www.census.gov/prod/2002pubs/p23-210.pdf.

Engle, J., & Tinto, V. (2008). "Moving Beyond Access: College Success For Low-Income, First-Generation Students." Pell Institute for the Study of Opportunity in Higher Education. Available: http://www.pellinstitute.org/files/COE_MovingBeyondReport_Final.pdf

"Education pays ..." (May 21, 2010). Bureau of Labor Statistics, Current Population Survey. Available: http://www.bls.gov/emp/ep_chart_001.htm

Franke, R., Ruiz, S., Sharkness, J., DeAngelo, L., & Pryor, J.P. (2010, February). "Findings from the 2009 Administration of the College Senior Survey (CSS): National Aggregates." Higher Education Research Institute. Available: http://www.heri.ucla.edu/PDFs/pubs/Reports/2009_CSS_Report.pdf

Gladwell, M. (2011, Feb. 14). "The Order of Things: What College Rankings Really Tell Us." The New Yorker, pp.68-89.

Hacker, A., & Dreifus, C. (2010). "Higher Education? How Colleges Are Wasting Our Money and Failing Our Kids – and What We Can Do About It." New York: Times Books.

Kantrowitz, M. (2010, Aug. 11). "Total College Debt Now Exceeds Total Credit Card Debt." Available: http://www.fastweb.com/financial-aid/articles/2589-total-college-debt-now-exceeds-total-credit-card-debt.

Knapp, L.G., Kelly-Reid, J.E., & Ginder, S.A. (2010). "Postsecondary Institutions and Price of Attendance in the United States: Fall 2009, Degrees and Other Awards Conferred: 2008–09, and 12-Month Enrollment: 2008–09" U.S. Department of Education. Washington, DC: National Center for Education Statistics. Available: http://nces.ed.gov/pubsearch.

Kuh, G., Kinzie, J., Schuh, J., Whitt, E., et al. (2005). "Student Success in College: Creating Conditions That Matter." San Francisco: Jossey-Bass.

Muraskin, L., & Lee, J., with Wilner, A., & Swail, W. (2004, December). "Raising the Graduation Rates of Low-Income College Students." Pell Institute for the Study of Opportunity in Higher Education. Available: http://www.luminafoundation.org/publications/PellDec2004.pdf

National Center for Education Statistics. U.S. Department of Education Institute of Education Sciences. Available: http://nces.ed.gov/

"Occupational Outlook Handbook, 2010-2011 Edition." Bureau of Labor Statistics. Available: www.bls.gov/oco/

Occupational Employment Statistics. Bureau of Labor Statistics. Available: www.bls.gov/oes/

Pope, L. (2006). "Colleges That Change Lives: 40 Schools That Will Change the Way You Think About Colleges." New York: Penguin Books.

"Private Loans: Facts & Trends." (2009, August). Project on Student Debt. Available: http://projectonstudentdebt.org/files/pub/private_loan_facts_trends_09.pdf

Pryor, J. H., Hurtado, S., DeAngelo, L., Palucki Blake, L., & Tran, S. (2010, January). "The American Freshman: National Norms for 2009." Higher Education Research Institute. Available: http://www.heri.ucla.edu/PDFs/pubs/briefs/HERI_ResearchBrief_Norms2010.pdf

"Quick Facts About Student Debt." (2010, January). Project on Student Debt: An Initiative of the Institute for College Access & Success. Available: http://projectonstudentdebt.org/files/File/Debt_Facts_and_Sources.pdf

Ruiz, S., Sharkness, J., Kelly, K., DeAngelo, L., & Pryor, J.H. (2010, January). "Findings from the 2009 Administration of the Your First College Year (YFCY): National Aggregates." Higher Education Research Institute. Available: http://www.heri.ucla.edu/PDFs/pubs/Reports/YFCY2009Final_January.pdf

"Student Persistence in College: More Than Counting Caps and Gowns." American Federation of Teachers. Available: http://faculty.irsc.edu/edp/Reading%20Room%20Articles/student_persistence.pdf

Supiano, B. (2010, Sep. 21). "Education Pays, but How Much?" Chronicle of Higher Education. Available: http://chronicle.com/article/article-content/124552/.

Taylor, M. (2010). "Crisis on Campus: A Bold Plan for Reforming Our Colleges and Universities." New York: Alfred A. Knopf.

Tinto, V. (2004, July). "Student Retention and Graduation: Facing the Truth, Living With the Consequences." Pell Institute for the Study of Opportunity in Higher Education. Available: http://www.pellinstitute.org/tinto/TintoOccasionalPaperRetention.pdf

"Trends in College Pricing 2010." Trends in Higher Education Series. College Board Advocacy & Policy Center. Available: http://trends.collegeboard.org/downloads/College_Pricing_2010.pdf

"Trends in College Pricing 2009." Trends in Higher Education Series. College Board. Available: http://trends.collegeboard.org/downloads/archives/CP_2009.pdf

"Trends in Student Aid 2010." Trends in Higher Education Series. College Board Advocacy & Policy Center. Available: http://trends.collegeboard.org/downloads/Student_Aid_2010.pdf

U.S. Census Bureau. Available: www.census.gov

Index

Symbols

About the Authors

Alice C. Stewart *(Ph.D., University of North Carolina-Chapel Hill)* teaches strategy and management at North Carolina A&T University. Over the past 30 years, she has taught in a wide variety of academic settings, from elite research institutions to small private colleges. Along the way, Alice has had the opportunity to turn her professional eye to her own industry – higher education. During her five years as Director of Strategic Analysis and Planning at The Ohio State University, Alice explored some of the underlying tensions universities face as they transition to institutions with higher student demand and higher expectations for economic impact and organizational accountability. In 2011, Alice's ability to articulate a new vision for business education was rewarded with first place in the Ideas to Innovation challenge, a global competition sponsored by the Graduate Management Admission Council. As a strategy professor, teaching and advising undergraduates, Alice has been inspired by students who have overcome the odds and disheartened by students who have overspent and under studied. Alice brings her insights from many years of day-to-day interactions with students to this book. She hopes that students and parents will take a more strategic, "big picture" view of the college decision and realize that in higher education *caveat emptor* prevails!

Fran Stewart is a Cleveland-area writer, editor and designer. She has spent more than 15 years working for newspapers, including the Cleveland *Plain Dealer*, where she wrote about personal finance issues. That's when she began to explore college choice in terms of its return on investment. In 2006, Fran helped found *College 101*, a twice yearly magazine for Ohio high school students. She has written in the areas of economic development, public policy and urban issues and has worked on projects for the State of Ohio, universities, a Cleveland-area think tank, a variety of non-profit organizations and the U.S. Department of Housing and Urban Development. Her first book, *In Their Path: A Grandmother's 519-Mile Underground Railroad Walk*, examined Ohio's abolitionist history. She is a founding member of Restore Cleveland Hope, a non-profit organization dedicated to saving a local historic building and highlighting Cleveland's Underground Railroad past.